Family Addictions

A Guide For Surviving Alcohol and Drug Abuse

by
Charles R. Norris Jr., M.D.

T·H·E
PIA
PRESS

19 Prospect Street
Summit, NJ 07901

This book is not intended to replace personal medical care and/or professional supervision; there is no substitute for the experience and information that your doctor or mental health professional can provide. Rather, it is our hope that this book will provide additional information to help people understand the nature of addiction and psychiatric conditions that can evolve.

Proper treatment should always be tailored to the individual. If you read something in this book that seems to conflict with your doctor or mental health professional's instructions, contact him/her. There may be sound reasons for recommending treatment that may differ from the information presented in this book.

If you have any questions about any treatment in this book, please consult your doctor or mental health care professional.

In addition, the names and cases used in this book do not represent actual people, but are composite cases drawn from several sources.

Books Available Through PIA Press

DEDICATION

To my parents who gave me the foundation to do the kind of work I do today; to my children—Charlie and Jackie—who bring joy to my life, and to my wife, Franchesca, who takes care of me in so many little ways.

ACKNOWLEDGMENT

I wish to gratefully acknowledge my treatment team— Sylvia, Peggy, Roxie, Jan, Jody, Hank, both Ricks, Harold, Don, Woody, Chris and both Pats—who have taught me much that has helped make this book possible. I am especially thankful for the tremendous contributions of Ron Schaumburg and Dan Montopoli for their assistance in this endeavor.

CONTENTS

CHAPTER 1 Addiction: A Family Problem......................1

CHAPTER 2 Codependency and Enabling......................15

CHAPTER 3 Denial and Other Defenses:
The Psychological Elements of
Addiction..30

CHAPTER 4 The Biology of Addiction 45

CHAPTER 5 When Intervention Is Necessary...............57

CHAPTER 6 Family Support in the Inpatient Setting...70

CHAPTER 7 Family Support Outside the Hospital.......84

CHAPTER 8 Working Together to Prevent Relapse.....101

CHAPTER 9 Special Needs in Family Therapy...........113

SOURCES...130

INDEX 134

Charles R. Norris, Jr., M.D., Director of Addiction Services, Fair Oaks Hospital, Dr. Norris is a Phi Beta Kappa graduate of Bates College and received his medical degree from the University of Vermont School of Medicine. He did his psychiatric residency training at the Institute of Living in Hartford, Connecticut. Following his residency, Dr. Norris served as Senior Staff Psychiatrist, Director of Adult Outpatient Services, and Director of Ambulatory Services at the Institute of Living, prior to joining the staff at Fair Oaks Hospital in Florida.

Dr. Norris is an experienced and skilled clinician who has worked extensively with patients with dual diagnosis problems (combined emotional and substance abuse problems).

Dr. Norris has worked extensively with impaired professionals and as a consultant to industrial and professional groups on substance problems. He has published and lectured on a variety of topics including: biology of cocaine dependence, cocaine dependence and the family, and diagnosing the dual diagnosis patient. He combines his expert training in and commitment to individual psychotherapy with his expertise in addiction in treating dual diagnosis patients.

Dr. Norris is Board Certified in Psychiatry by the American Board of Psychiatry and Neurology, and is a member of the American Academy of Psychiatrists in Alcoholism and Addictions.

CHAPTER 1

ADDICTION:
A FAMILY PROBLEM

Perry* strode into my office and greeted me with a flashy smile and a firm handshake. At age 29, Perry was a successful salesman working for an insurance company. Smart, outgoing, and energetic, Perry was a born salesman.

And a drug addict.

For a moment, I thought it was strange that this young man had sunk so far that he had to enter our hospital in Florida for help. He was good-looking, capable, earning a six-figure income. If you saw him on the street, you'd think he had everything going for him.

Then I remembered why he was here.

You see, a while back the police in Perry's home state of Maryland stopped him for speeding. Luckily he hadn't hurt anyone, but as they searched his car, the

---

* Patient names and identifying characteristics have been changed to protect patient privacy.

cops spotted a tiny glass vial, the kind typically used to contain rocks of crack cocaine. A further search turned up a few more vials—full ones—in his jacket pocket. Perry was busted for possession. But let him tell the rest:

"They threw me in jail. No one wanted to bail me out. My father said maybe this would teach me a lesson. See, when I was living at home he had caught me smoking pot plenty of times. He never did anything about it, but he always said, 'One day you'll be sorry.' He's got problems of his own, anyway—he's a real flake, you know, moody. My brother, he deals drugs—I often get mine from him—and he wasn't about to set foot in a police station. And my mother died a few years ago. So I had to deal with this alone.

"Then it struck me—I'd seen this in some old movie somewhere. If I wanted to get out of jail, all I had to do was act crazy. So I started beating my arms against the wall of the cell. And I mean *hard*. All the other inmates started screaming and yelling. It was hysterical. I was all bloody, my cellmate was cowering in a corner. Finally the guards came and dragged me out of there. I remember as I left the cell one of the other cons slowly clapped his hands—you know, applauding my little act. He knew what I was doing. I thought it would hurt more, bashing my arms like that, but it didn't. Not really.

"Well, that got me out of jail and into a psych ward at some hospital. It was more comfortable, anyway. They tried to cure me. I was there—I don't know, three or four months. After I got out I stayed clean for a while, but I felt pretty down. Then I read that the Grateful Dead were going to be playing a concert in San Francisco. I started to feel ecstatic. I'm a true Deadhead—I'd follow them anywhere. So I hopped a plane out of Dulles and went to the show. Naturally, there were lots of drugs available at the concert. I got high for the first time in a couple of months. I knew from the first snort of coke that I was hooked again. All that treatment—*pfffft*, out the window."

This cycle repeated itself several times over a couple of years. "Things would be zooming along—sales were great, commissions were high. I'd get extra money to spend, so I'd blow it on drugs, overdo it a little, then crash. During those down times I was pretty useless—depressed, no energy, couldn't close a sale. I was in and out of treatment programs. They might as well have put revolving doors on those hospitals. I would go in, stay for a while, come out, go back on drugs, go back into treatment. Finally I thought, what I need is a change of scenery."

Perry called his grandfather, who lives here in Florida, and said he wanted to come and stay for a while. I have to give Grandpa Mike credit. He's a retired Washington, D.C., cop who has seen drugs destroy a lot of people. He wanted to have a chance at helping his grandson. So he told Perry to come down. But when Perry arrived, the grandfather told him not to bother unpacking. He'd enrolled Perry in the treatment program here at Fair Oaks Hospital.

Perry scoffed, "I've been through lots of programs. They don't work."

The grandfather replied, "You're going to try one more."

That's when Perry came to see me. In the six weeks that followed some remarkable things happened. We tested Perry and found out that he suffered from a disorder in brain chemistry that resulted in sudden mood shifts. A medication called lithium helped him regulate those moods. Equally important, we were able to get his fiance and sister to agree to fly down and take part in some family therapy sessions, along with the grandfather.

In those sessions they learned about the nature of Perry's addiction and how they may have contributed to the severity of the problem through their own actions and attitudes. The father, for example, saw how tolerating his son's marijuana use enabled him to fall further into addiction. Together we discovered ways the family might act to help Perry stay off drugs once he left the hospital. And Perry's brother was so impressed with the improvement in Perry that he also entered treatment for his drug problem.

That was two years ago. Recently I ran into Perry's grandfather, who attended a speech I gave about drug addiction at a community center. He told me that the way Perry has turned his life around is "miraculous." Perry is married, has a son, and has become involved in community antidrug programs. He is closer with his relatives than ever, because they no longer engage in behavior that reinforces his tendency to use drugs. His career is progressing smoothly now that, thanks to medication, he doesn't suffer long periods of low mood that interfere with his efforts at selling. He also doesn't experience periods of extreme high mood, which in the past caused him to seek thrills and take chances, such as smoking crack.

As Perry himself observed, "It's a lot easier to coast through life when the road is level than when it's all peaks and valleys."

THE PRESSURE IS ON

Perry's story reflects many of the main themes I'll discuss throughout the rest of this book. Like many other addicts, his drug problem was the result of pressure coming from three directions:

- the risk, to a large extent inherited, that he might develop some kind of psychiatric disorder, including addiction;
- his own thrill-seeking behavior, caused in part by a biochemical imbalance and reinforced by his experiences with drugs; and
- pressure from his social environment—his work as a salesman in a high-anxiety field, the drug subculture with which he associated himself, and unhealthy attitudes about drug use encountered at home and in society.

Perry's story also shows how treatment for drug problems is never complete unless it addresses such key issues as the need for intervention, the danger of relapse, and the possibility that other mental problems are contributing to drug use.

Finally, Perry's case dramatizes how drug use affects not just the addict himself, but everyone around him. Some so-called "experts" argue that drug use should be tolerated, even legalized, because it is a "victimless" crime. *Wrong*. Drugs affect more than just the person who takes them. They also have a devastating impact on the addict's parents, spouse, children, employers, and friends. Only when we see the drug user as part of this larger system and apply treatment to as many aspects of that system as possible, will we stand a chance of freeing patients from the tyranny of drugs.

In the last few years, we have realized how critical it is to involve the family in every step of the addict's treatment and recovery. Even more important, the best caregiving facilities have incorporated that awareness into their treatment programs. The result is that drug treatment is now more effective than ever before.

If you are wrestling with drug addiction in your family, this book will show you what your role will be in breaking the cycle. You'll learn about:

Codependency—how other members of the family act in ways that reinforce the addict's drug-using behavior.

Intervention—when to step in, how to confront the addict about the problem, how to get the addict into treatment.

Support during in-hospital treatment—understanding therapy, taking part in family therapy sessions.

Support after the patient is released—how to make changes at home and in your own behavior to reinforce the effects of treatment.

Relapse prevention—how relapse is a constant risk, how to act to minimize the likelihood of relapse.

Recovery—the lifelong process of getting better; the value of Twelve-Step Programs such as Alcoholics Anonymous, Al-Anon, Nar-Anon, and other programs that address the needs of the family.

WHAT IS A FAMILY?

Here's a little word association test: What do you think of when you hear the word "family"? Father, mother, 2.2 kids, station wagon in the garage of a suburban home? I suppose if you looked hard enough you'd find some families that do fit that stereotype.

In reality, though, the family is not what it used to be. Divorce rates are high; while approximately two and a half million couples get married each year, over a million couples get divorced. Other couples separate. When you include remarriage, death, and other factors, you'd be hard pressed to find examples of the intact nuclear family—the clichéd *Leave It to Beaver* family of thirty or forty years ago.

Today, when we say "family," we may mean a mother and her children, the father having skipped out long ago. Some families consist of children who are being raised by older relatives, such as grandparents. This is often the case when addiction seizes hold of a young mother who abandons her children in favor of drugs or alcohol. Families where couples remarry may have any number of siblings and half-siblings. In some cases there can be an enormous gap in the ages of children from the first marriage and those from the second.

The patient may be a husband whose drug use has drained the family savings account and jeopardized the family's financial future. Or the patient may be a woman with a childhood history of being abused physically or sexually. Or it may be a woman who feels trapped in her role as housewife and who, alone all day in an empty house, turns to drugs for solace. It may be an unmarried couple who live together and are only now discovering the dark side of each other's personality. Or it may be a partner in a homosexual relationship who urges the other to get help, especially given the increased risk of AIDS among users of intravenous drugs. Each of these situations involves a family of one kind or another.

Within a recent six-month period I handled the following cases:

- A man being treated in the hospital who was served with divorce papers from his wife *and* a restraining order preventing him from seeing his girlfriend—*on the same day*.
- A woman who was ordered into treatment by a court that convicted her of child abuse because she smoked crack up to the day she delivered her baby.
- A 72-year-old "child" who insisted that her 96-year-old father get treatment for alcoholism because she feared he would fall and break his hip.

My point is that each situation is different; each family faces unique challenges.

The problem involves not just conflict between the sexes but among the generations as well. Parents may be concerned about their adolescent son or daughter. As we saw in Perry's case, it was actually the grandfather who found a treatment program for his grandson. With the growing awareness among our culture of the need for drug treatment, many adult children are steering their parents—some of whom are elderly—into therapy.

If you are seeking help for someone with a drug problem, *be sure the treatment program is designed to address family issues*. Equally important, be sure the program recognizes that your family has its own special needs. Programs that use a cookie-cutter, one-size-fits-all approach to treatment will do no good for the patient or for concerned relatives. This book will tell you what to look for in a treatment program.

The good news is that, regardless of age, family structure, and past relationships, help is available. Be assured: No matter how complicated your life has become, no matter how long your loved one has been addicted to drugs or alcohol, no matter how hopeless you may feel, *therapy can help.*

SYSTEMS

You're driving down the street and suddenly the car's engine blows. The mechanics look it over. They say something like, "Your whoozits melted because a rock got caught in the whatzis and stopped the doohickey from turning." They remove the engine and fix the problem, but of course the job isn't done until they've replaced the engine, reconnected the hoses and wires, and made sure the whole car is working.

As with a mechanical failure, a combination of events may lead a person to break down and succumb to drug addiction. Admitting the patient to the hospital allows the treatment team to focus on the person who needs help most. But sooner or later that person must be reconnected to the family, the workplace, the society. We learn how effective therapy has been only after the patient leaves the hospital and reenters the "real world."

That's why I believe in the *systems approach* to treatment for drug problems. Working with others on the caregiving team, I assess my patients to learn how they operate within, and are affected by, the many larger systems that shape their lives. I explore to see where those systems may have broken down and thus contributed to the severity of the problem. Once we have identified the troublesome areas—lack of communication among family members, for example—we can work out solutions.

Some people refer to this way of looking at drug addiction as the *biopsychosocial model*. This jaw-breaking term is really just a way of highlighting the key elements that contribute to drug abuse and to many other psychiatric illnesses. Let's break the word down into its parts.

"Bio-" refers to the biological factors: genetic inheritance from one's parents; the impact of drugs on the body; other illnesses, such as depression, that may cause people to try and treat themselves through use of illicit drugs.

"-psych" means the patient's psychological traits that may fan the flames of drug use. For example, a person may learn early in life that she could do something wrong, blame her little brother for it, and get away scot-free. If she succeeds in this little gambit often enough, it becomes an ingrained part of her behavior—a kind of survival mechanism that, once learned, becomes self-reinforcing. The pattern will persist even as she progresses into adulthood. In a drug addict, the habit of blaming someone else might emerge in the form of denial: "I don't have a drug problem, I'm just under a lot of pressure from my boss." I'll have more to say about denial later in the book. The point is that a person's psychology—that unique combination of life experiences, emotions, thought patterns, and behavior—adds its own fuel to the fire of drug addiction.

The *"social"* part refers to the patient's interactions with other people at home, at work, and in society. Obviously a person whose friends are heavy drug users is more likely to use drugs too. Similarly, having a drug-using sibling, spouse, or "significant other" is one of the highest risk factors. For many years our culture was tolerant of drug use—movies and TV programs glorified drugs, depicting them as sources of fun and hilarity. The point is that the general cultural climate contributes to an individual's drug-using behavior.

I'm happy to say that all signs point to a huge shift in our attitudes: Drug-free school zones, tough laws, less tolerant attitudes about drugs, dropping rates of drug use among high school students—all of these point to a renewed commitment to the drug-free lifestyle. As a physician, I can only hope that as lowered tolerance for drugs becomes the norm in our society, I'll have fewer addicted patients to treat. As a realist, though, I know there is still much to be done, and that my hospital ward will be full for many years to come.

THERAPY AS EDUCATION

Like Perry, many of the patients I see have been through treatment before. Some have entered ten or more therapy programs. They get out, stay clean for a while, then relapse so severely that they have to get help again. Thus, when their families bring them to me, they don't usually ask, "What are you going to do?" Instead they want to know, "What are you going to do that hasn't been tried half a dozen times before?"

Sometimes, the answer is surprisingly simple: By teaching them the facts about addiction, we educate them in ways that help the patient—and the family members—eliminate behaviors and attitudes that contribute to drug use. We give them the tools they need to fight addiction, the tools that allow their own motivation to stop using drugs to flourish.

Sometimes we identify a patient's underlying psychiatric problem, such as depression or anxiety. These underlying psychiatric problems are often masked by substance abuse. Once uncovered, these psychiatric problems usually respond well to treatment.

Invariably we find that families in which drug use is a problem have severe difficulty communicating with each other. The basic trouble is that they let their emotions get in the way. Most people haven't had much training in how to deal with their emotions. Many times parents, inadvertently or not, teach their children to hide their feelings: "Don't cry! Only sissies cry!" Or, "You don't like the chores you have to do around this house? Tough luck—maybe you should move out!" Or, "Come on, dive in the water already! What are you, a scaredy-cat?" When children who have been taught to suppress their feelings become adults, they lack the tools they need to recognize a genuine emotion and to express it in appropriate and healthy ways.

Why should this be the case? Why do families fail to teach each other this fundamental lesson in survival?

To my way of thinking, the answer is found in the changes—many of them negative changes—that the family has undergone in the past three decades. It would take half a dozen books to describe these trends: families where both parents must work due to financial pressure; corporations who demand more from their employees at the expense of family life; increased opportunities for women that reduce their time at home; children given over to babysitters or day care for perhaps 12 hours a day.

To compensate, many families make a special effort to see that the precious time spent together is rich and rewarding—the so-called "quality time" we hear about. They make dinner a festive occasion, with lively conversation and rollicking banter. They reserve weekends exclusively for family activities. Other families, however, don't make this effort. If they eat together at all, they do so in front of a flickering TV screen. The conversation and banter comes from a game show host and his contestants; the laughter is canned. There isn't any time to learn about each other's thoughts and feelings.

When children grow up, they tend to repeat the patterns they learned early in life. That's only natural; children imitate what they see. If the family is struggling to cope with alcoholism, then the child learns to lie, to hide feelings, to deny the reality.

The majority of my patients come from dysfunctional families where at least one of the parents is an alcoholic. These people thus inherit a genetic tendency toward substance abuse—the "*bio*" part of the biopsychosocial model. And they grow up in an atmosphere of tension, bitterness, and pain—the "*social*" factor. Unless they learn the skills they need to resist these powerful forces, they risk turning to drugs or alcohol to relieve their own stressful feelings—the "*psych*" part.

We teach our patients and their families that, for the most part, *addiction is addiction*. To a treatment specialist like myself, a cocaine dependency is not too much different from an alcohol dependency—only the course of the illness varies.

We also stress that *addiction is a disease*. It is not the result of emotional weakness or moral failure.

Another key point is that, for many patients, *addiction may be a symptom of an underlying psychiatric disorder*. In Perry's case, we found he was suffering from a bipolar mood disorder—the technical name for mood swings. Many other patients have some form of depression or personality problem. Often we find that treating these underlying conditions goes a long way in relieving the problem of substance abuse.

Lastly, *recovery from addiction is a lifelong process*. Patients need constant help to avoid returning to their

old habits and patterns. That's where the strength and
support of the family becomes most crucial. Many drug
treatment centers also offer ongoing therapy that reinforces the work done while the patient was in the hospital. And the guidance offered by the Twelve-Step programs
such as AA is absolutely invaluable to the recovering
addict. I'll have more to say about each of these topics
later in this book.

In a sense, recovering addicts are involved in a kind
of "love triangle." One side of that triangle consists of
caring therapists—doctors, social workers, and counselors. Another side consists of supportive self-help groups
made up of people who have suffered from dependency
and who are working to overcome their troubled past
one day at a time.

The third side, of equal importance, is the love given
by the family. As this book will show, by helping your
addicted relative get help and by learning about your
crucial role in the process of recovery, you will be
expressing your love in the healthiest and most healing
way possible.

CHAPTER 2

CODEPENDENCY
AND ENABLING

During his therapy for cocaine addiction, Allen worked very hard. He attended all the group sessions, cooperated with the programs in every detail, and was a model patient. Nonetheless, at the end of the treatment program, he felt he wasn't quite ready to reenter society completely. He was particularly concerned about returning to his parents' home, because his father was a severe alcoholic who had refused to take part in family therapy sessions at the hospital. Allen wanted to enter a halfway house—a live-in community of people who are still wrestling with addiction but who offer each other lots of mutual support as they continue to recover.

Allen called his mother and asked her to send $250 to pay for a room at the halfway house. I got on the phone and told his mother, "Be sure and make the check out to the house, not to your son." The next day the check came by Federal Express—payable to Allen. He signed himself out of the hospital, cashed the check, and made a beeline for his drug dealer.

Within an hour after leaving treatment, Allen was once again smoking crack.

Did we fail in our efforts to treat Allen? On the surface, it would certainly appear so. Even in the best of cases, relapse is a constant risk, but it's particularly painful when a patient completes the program, walks out the door, and—*boom*—gets lost in a drug-induced fog.

Can we blame Allen for being weak, a hopeless case? Not really. Remember, many addicts use drugs for years before seeking help. That's a lot of time in which a habit can become deeply ingrained. To expect an addict to overcome a problem with severe physical, emotional, and mental complications in one short month—even a month of intensive therapy—is expecting a great deal.

As his physician, I accept responsibility for what happened to Allen. Nonetheless, in my defense, I name as my "co-culprit" Allen's mother.

Despite my specific instructions to the contrary, the mother put money in the hands of her recovering son. As one of my colleagues phrased it, "That's like giving a Zippo lighter to an arsonist." By enabling him to run right out and buy drugs, she completely undermined everyone's efforts to save him from disaster.

The key word in that last sentence is "enabling." By her actions, the mother created a situation that permitted the problem to continue. Did she do so deliberately? No. But sometimes an inadvertent slip can result in just as great a tragedy as a deliberate act of sabotage.

GROWING AWARENESS OF CODEPENDENCY

In the past few years the terms enabling and codependency have dominated much of the discussion about addiction. Many books have been written on the subject; some of them have stayed on the bestseller lists for months. You may have even read one or two of these yourself in your struggle to find ways of helping your addicted loved one.

As is often the case when a trendy new concept catches on, a lot of people have jumped on the codependency bandwagon. Now that the subject has trickled down to the level of the supermarket tabloids, I'm concerned that a lot of misinformation about what codependency really is will lead to more confusion.

Recently, for example, we admitted a 27-year-old woman for treatment for alcohol addiction. About two weeks into the program, her father stormed into my office waving a newspaper. "This article says that everybody in an alcoholic's family is a codependent. I've never had a drink in my life. I will not allow myself to be tarred with that brush." He demanded that his daughter be released. Eventually we were able to calm him down and explain that codependency does not necessarily mean that relatives of an addict are themselves addicted.

Here's another case: The Millers had pleaded with their son for several years to get help for his problem with marijuana and alcohol. Finally, after his life fell apart, he agreed. They enrolled him in our program. The day before he was to come into the hospital they called and said they were cancelling. They had just read a book about codependency and had somehow gotten the idea that drug treatment programs brainwashed addicts into thinking that everyone else was to "blame" for their problem. "We love our son, in spite of his trouble. We won't let you turn him against us," they said angrily, and hung up.

If you feel confused, you're not alone, as these anecdotes illustrate. Let me try to explain these two concepts as clearly as I can. Perhaps the best way is to show how the concepts, and our understanding, have evolved in recent years.

THE EVOLUTION OF CODEPENDENCY

Generally, our understanding of codependent behavior emerged from the valuable work done by the Twelve-Step programs such as AA. Over the years, as members shared their stories of their past and present experiences, certain patterns began to emerge. It became clear that families with a substance-abusing member operated by certain more or less overt rules, rules that tended to precipitate and reinforce chemical dependency. Hence the name codependency.

People thus began to identify a basic problem—so far, so good. But for many years there was no solution to that problem. Treatment and self-help support centered, as it had to, on the person with the addiction. Where, though, was help to be found for those who loved that person but who didn't know how to break their old enabling habits?

What we've seen in the past decade or so is essentially a grass-roots movement in which the people who needed help rose up and demanded it. As some have put it, the health-care consumers got together, gave their problem a name, and demanded that health-care givers find some answers.

In the process the terms codependency and enabling

were redefined. At first, a codependent was simply the child, parent, spouse, or significant other of the addicted person. By the mid-1970s, codependency was seen as a dysfunctional pattern of living arising from a set of problematic rules by which a family operated. Currently, as I indicated earlier, we think of codependency as a pattern that, like addiction, results from physical, psychological, and cultural pressure. That pressure produces individuals whose identity is so tied in to the problems of their loved ones that they essentially stop growing and devote themselves instead to preserving the sick system in which they operate.

Codependency, by whatever definition, involves other people. Thus I see it as basically the *social* element of the biopsychosocial model of addiction that I mentioned in the previous chapter. We'll focus on the "*psych*" and "*bio*" elements in chapter 3 and 4.

Some experts make a strong case for looking at codependency as a clear-cut, diagnosable psychiatric illness. As we've seen, there are certain symptoms, certain patterns of thought and behavior, that seem to emerge with predictable frequency. And, as I'll show later in this book, there are therapies that can work wonders in breaking the chains of codependency and freeing families from their dysfunctional patterns.

In talking with patients, and in question-and-answer sessions following my speeches to the public, I've often heard people challenge the view of codependency as an illness. "You're a shrink," one man said. "It's in your best interests if you go around saying that everyone in a substance abuser's family needs help, too. You wind up with an endless supply of patients that way."

I certainly understand that criticism. But I try to point out that we psychiatrists didn't invent the diagnosis—

our patients did. Many of those in my profession were blind to both addiction and codependency for so many years. What happened was that thousands of people were suffering and didn't know why. When they banded together and looked closely at what was happening to themselves and their families, they found a sick cycle of behavior. They then turned to medical professionals to help them find answers. In the years that followed, scientific research validated what the public had told us was true: Treating addiction is only half the battle. Discharging patients from treatment back into an unhealthy environment is like curing people of malaria and sending them back into the jungle. The chance of reinfection is extremely high.

CODEPENDENCY AND ENABLING: A DEFINITION

Codependents are people who tend to base their identity, their whole sense of self, on their ability to take care of other people. They dedicate themselves to others whom they perceive to be needier. And who could be needier than a person caught in the throes of addiction? That's why codependents are found so often in relationships with substance abusers. Something draws them to form partnerships with people in desperate need of help. Some experts claim that codependents suppress their own personal needs in order to help others. This isn't strictly true. By devoting themselves to "saving" an addicted individual, codependents actually gratify their most basic desire: their need to be needed.

There are two sides to codependency. On the positive side, yes, addicts do need help, and the best person to give that help is someone who cares about them deeply. Codependents are loving people. What we do in family therapy is try to show those people how to use their love to help the addict get well.

On the negative side, in order to feel fulfilled, a codependent has to be involved with someone who needs help. Obviously if the addict manages to go straight, the codependent is left without a job, so to speak. On one level a wife might say, "I don't want my husband to drink." But on another level she's thinking, If he weren't drinking he wouldn't need to be taken care of, and thus he might not need me any more. The trouble comes when the codependent, unaware of this very real risk, begins to act in ways that scuttle the patient's efforts to get better.

Enabling, simply put, is what codependents do. Enabling refers to the behavior of people who, more or less subconsciously and in order to gratify their own needs, would rather their addicted relative keep right on drinking and drugging.

Here are some classic enabling behaviors: An addict goes on a binge and passes out on the floor. His wife manages to get him into bed and cleans up his mess. The next morning he's too sick to go to work, so she calls the boss and says her husband has the flu. A week later the addict gets stopped for drunk driving. The wife leaves work to bail him out. His boss, fed up with the addict's behavior, fires him. The wife agrees to support the family, working overtime and drawing from her trust fund, "just until he feels better."

To one degree or another, all codependents are enablers, at least in the beginning. Perhaps Jack sees that Jill, a crack addict, needs help; fulfilling his fantasy of rescuing the fair maiden, Jack marries her. Their attraction, however, is based almost exclusively on his unhealthy desire to take care of another person and her unhealthy need to be taken care of rather than stand on her own two feet. If Jill stops using drugs, the marriage loses its focus.

Sometimes substance abusers manage to keep their drug use a secret, even from their spouses, for many years. Or the codependent—like the addict—may deny the existence of a problem. Confronted with a deteriorating situation, the spouse may struggle to make excuses: "Her drinking's not that bad—after all she's never passed out," or, "I know he'll stop completely—just as soon as he has a real job."

CODEPENDENCY IN ACTION

Let me cite some real-life examples. During a conversation with a patient's husband, I asked how his wife had usually acquired her cocaine. "Oh, I buy it for her," said Bart. My eyes betrayed my surprise. Bart went on: "I know she's going to buy drugs anyway. I figure this way at least I can control the amount that comes into the house. Besides, I think it's safer. She doesn't have to deal with that scum, and I'm tough enough that the pushers won't try to mess with me." As you might imagine, at that point I steered the discussion toward the subject of enabling.

As I said earlier, a person can be a codependent without ever using drugs or alcohol. In some cases, though, a codependent can indeed be coaddicted. I've treated many couples who slid into addiction together. For example, over the years following his divorce, Jerry fell into the habit of downing a couple of Scotches every night after dinner. When he remarried, he insisted that Louise join him in this practice. She was reluctant at first, but eventually she got used to the idea. Soon she was keeping up with him, drink for drink. It got to the point where they would have weekend drinking contests to see who could down the most booze before passing out.

Here's another example. Chuck first met Laura at a party; they were both snorting lines of cocaine from the same mirror. They continued to get together for what they called "coke dates," a not-so-funny reference to the innocent soda shop dates their parents had enjoyed in the fifties. They began living together. They soon "graduated" to crack.

After a few years, though, Laura began feeling burned out and wanted to get off drugs. She asked Chuck not to bring crack home any more. Every Friday— payday—she'd call and remind him, "Now don't buy any more of that stuff. Remember I'm trying to quit." But the temptation was always too great. After cashing his check he'd stop by the crack house and do some business. He'd come home high, with crack vials clinking in his pockets. "That clinking sound was like Pavlov's bell," Laura said. "I'd hear it and start drooling. I wanted crack." They'd smoke the rest of the weekend. Finally she brought herself into the hospital for treatment, but Chuck refused to join her. "I don't need help," he said. "I can quit anytime."

Laura was a good patient. She worked hard. She eventually persuaded Chuck to attend family therapy sessions in the evenings. Interestingly, it was at those sessions that Chuck saw how determined Laura was to quit, and saw for himself the importance of getting off drugs. A few weeks after she was discharged, Laura returned for a followup consultation and reported that

Chuck had stopped smoking crack. I was of course pleased to hear the news and congratulated her for setting such a good example for her codependent. I tried to caution her, however, that Chuck hadn't gone through the same kind of treatment program that had given her such a solid basis for getting better, and that relapse was highly probable. We're keeping our fingers crossed, but the latest report was still encouraging.

PARENTS AS ENABLERS

Earlier we saw how Perry's father served as an enabler. Here are some other ways parents inadvertently enable their children to use drugs.

Recently a physician friend of mine told me of a conversation he had with a high school principal. The principal said she had caught one of her students smoking marijuana on the campus and called the parents in for a conference. When she broke the news, the parents were chagrined. "I don't believe it," the mother said. "This is terrible." The principal started to mutter some words of reassurance, but the mother went on: "We *told* Wendy she could only smoke grass on weekends, and only in her own bedroom!"

Here were parents who knew about their daughter's use of drugs and who thought they were handling the problem by setting firm limits. In reality all they were doing was *enabling* her to develop her habit. Mom and Dad tried to send a clear signal about controlling drugs, but the message their daughter received was, "Drugs are okay." That's enabling.

One father told me he'd given his kid a good chewing out when he came home two hours after his curfew and smelling of booze. I pressed for details. The father said, "I bawled him out about being late and told him if it happened again he couldn't use the car for a month." Did he say anything about the drinking—or, even more important, the drinking and driving? "No." We spent the rest of our conversation talking about enabling.

Marta was a good student with a high grade average. One semester she brought home a report card showing poor marks in her favorite subject. When asked about it, she said, "My teacher hates me. I want to transfer to another class." The parents confronted the teacher, who said, "How can I teach Marta anything when she's either absent or asleep in class? Rumors are that she and her friends skip out to smoke pot." The parents confronted Marta, who went into a tantrum: "You believe *her* instead of me?" The parents placated their daughter, called the principal, and insisted Marta be transferred to another class. A month later the school district ordered a surprise search of student's lockers; in Marta's they found an ounce of marijuana. By ignoring some classic warning signs—change in performance at school, sleepiness, hanging out with the wrong crowd— Marta's parents denied the reality and took on the role of enablers.

You can see why I place such a high value on family therapy as an aspect of drug treatment. If we caregivers do our best, and if our patients make a commitment to get better, we can do some good work at healing the damage that has been done. But if we then release those patients into a home filled with people who need to have a sick person around in order to justify their own existence, or who are afraid to confront the problem head-on— then, friends, "we've got trouble right here in River City."

OTHER SOCIAL FACTORS IN CODEPENDENCY

Our primary focus in this chapter has been on the family of the addicted individual. Before I close this chapter I want to touch briefly on some of the other social factors that contribute to the problem.

Friends can be the addict's worst enemies. Those good ol' buddies who invite the alcoholic to join them to "hoist a few" after work are doing no one any favors. Friends who are threatened by a friend's abstinence may subtly act as enablers. Walt, a recovering alcoholic patient, told me how much subtle pressure his best friend could exert. This friend knew about Walt's condition and he never openly questioned Walt's abstinence. Instead, he would frequently recall "the good old days when you and me would 'party hearty'—boy, you were a lot of fun *then*." And of course, this "friend" would replay every detail of his latest drinking binge, carefully editing out the hangovers and blackouts. "Talk about waving a red flag," Walt remarked. "I'd sit there being a good boy listening to this and shaking my head. It wasn't long before I went with him to a bar. It was great, too. I did have a blast, just like before. Then the next day, the next morning I realized that it *was* just like before, just like all the things that I couldn't stand in myself and in my life. That night was the last time I ever saw my 'friend.' I never returned his calls, never spoke to him again. Funny thing, I haven't had a drink since then either."

Employers often miss the opportunity to help their workers. They may blind themselves to the problems of absenteeism, poor job performance, or high insurance costs because of frequent illness or accidents. Although employee assistance programs are widely available to help workers with drug problems, many employers refuse to offer them. They pile one excuse on top of another: "It's too expensive." "We don't need it." "I don't have junkies and winos working in *my* company."

And employers may ignore the drug problems of a close friend or relative who works for them, especially if this person is also an upper-level executive within the company. In fact, these employees are often the most protected employees in the company, with secretaries and supervisors both acting to cover up the employee's problem.

Community leaders sometimes fail to take initiatives that might help the people in their own neighborhood. I'm surprised, for example, at how some members of the clergy are unaware of their ability to help the people in their congregations confront drug abuse. Recently I spoke to an audience of ministers and rabbis on this very subject. Afterward, a minister approached me and said that his own daughter was an addict. He felt deeply ashamed, he said, not because he was embarrassed in front of his parishioners but because he had been blind to suffering in his own house. As he put it, "Sometimes we keep our eyes on heaven but are blind to what lies before us in the gutter." Many times I hear politicians brag about how much good they've done for their cities or states, then realize that they are ignoring the unpleasant facts about drug abuse in their communities.

Medical professionals, alas, are also not immune. Surprisingly, some doctors even in this age will examine a patient who is fatigued, undernourished, prone to respiratory and other infections—and still fail to ask even the most superficial questions about their use of illicit drugs or alcohol. Some emergency-room physicians will examine a patient complaining of chest pains and never even consider drug use. When the heart-attack tests prove negative, they'll usually attribute the chest pain to stress or anxiety. And some of those who do take a history of drug use fail to test the patient's blood or urine to verify the patient's answers. Conversely, some of my colleagues in addiction treatment will focus exclusively on the symptoms of drug use and fail to look for a deeper, underlying cause of the patient's behavior. In many cases patients have been referred to me for addiction treatment when it turns out their underlying problem is that they are medicating themselves in an effort to treat severe biological depression.

The thread that connects each of these cases is *denial*. We will return to this topic repeatedly throughout this book. Denial is one of the most difficult problems associated with addiction. Addicts deny they have a problem with chemical dependency. Spouses deny their mates are hooked. Children deny that there's anything wrong at home. Friends deny what they see. Employers deny that they might have an alcoholic on their staff. Community leaders blind themselves to problems. Doctors— who should be among the first to suspect trouble—fail to turn over this rock for fear of what might crawl out.

By promoting, glamorizing, and tolerating the use of drugs and alcohol, our society is one of the largest enablers of addiction. But from what I see, the situation is changing for the better. I credit those perceptive and persistent people who lobbied to raise our awareness of addiction and codependency. Today our society is less willing to ignore or tolerate the problems of drug use than it was a decade ago.

The wide publicity given to codependency has made the word a household term—and the household is *exactly* where it should be discussed and wrestled with. And, ironically, by teaching addicts and their families about the dark side of enabling, we show them the bright side: We enable them to break their sick patterns and replace them with healthy ones.

CHAPTER 3

DENIAL AND OTHER DEFENSES: THE PSYCHOLOGICAL ELEMENTS OF ADDICTION

Not long ago I saw someone wearing a T-shirt with a message that read: "I don't have a drinking problem. I drink, I get drunk, I fall down—no problem."

The shirt was supposed to be funny. I didn't think it was. As a doctor who treats people whose lives have been shattered by drugs and alcohol, I guess I don't have much of a sense of humor about such things.

In reality, the message on that T-shirt underscores one of the most serious and troublesome aspects of addiction: the problem of denial. Denial occurs when people caught up in addiction—not just the drug users, but their codependents as well—deliberately ignore the evidence that drugs or alcohol are ruining their lives. Thus the "joke" on the T-shirt: "I may be falling-down drunk, but, hey, it's no problem." Wanna bet?

Denial is serious, but it is just one of the many strategies that addicts use to block out the truth about their condition. Collectively, these strategies make up the psychological part—the *"psych"* part—of the biopsychosocial model of addiction. If you want to help your addicted loved one get better, you have to learn how to recognize these strategies, understand why and how the addict uses them, and discover the techniques for overcoming them.

DEFENSIVE STRATEGIES

Addicts have an amazing array of tricks up their sleeve. They use these tricks to cover up the severity of their problem or distract other people's attention from it. For the most part these psychological strategies—sometimes known as *defense mechanisms*—represent people's unconscious efforts to protect themselves against intolerable anxiety or emotional conflict.

Defense mechanisms fall into three basic categories: behavioral, cognitive, and emotional. Let me explain what I mean by these terms.

Behavioral strategies are the things addicts do to prevent other people from becoming aware of their problem or to protect their "right" to remain addicted. For example, addicts spend enormous amounts of energy protecting their supply of chemicals: hiding bottles of booze throughout the house, making up elaborate ruses as they go out to buy drugs, and so on.

Cognitive strategies are the "mind games" addicts

play on themselves and others. In many cases it takes some pretty twisted thinking for an addict to keep on using drugs despite the pain and suffering they cause. One of my patients, for example, told me he felt he had to keep using cocaine because it enhanced his perform- ance on the job. "If I didn't get tanked up with coke," he said, "I'd never be able to put in those long hours or concentrate on a demanding project." This patient had to convince himself that he needed coke in order to work, when in reality he was working overtime in order to pay for his drug habit.

Emotional strategies are those used by addicts to manipulate people into accepting their drug problem. One patient told me that whenever his wife started nagging him about his use of marijuana, he would pout and whine, even burst into tearful tantrums. When she backed off, he would turn friendly, playful, and charm- ing. As his wife said during a family therapy session, "I don't know which Ben is the real one." Another patient is extremely likeable and entertaining when high, but miserable when straight.

Let's look at some of these strategies in more detail.

DENIAL: PUBLIC HEALTH ENEMY #1

Recently I gave a speech about addiction. During the question-and-answer session someone remarked, "You said that addicts often deny they have a drug problem. But if you went up to a person who had never used drugs or booze in his life and you told that person, 'You have a drug problem,' he'd deny it, too, and he'd be right. How can you tell the difference between that kind of denial and the denial of addiction?"

I replied, "The person who is truly not addicted would respond by saying something like, 'Why do you think I have a drug problem?' The addict, on the other hand, would immediately give you a list of a dozen reasons to prove that he *isn't* addicted." The addict, in other words, would launch into the full-scale counteroffensive known as denial.

If you have tried to confront a loved one about his or her addiction, you have no doubt already run headlong into the brick wall of denial. Do any of these comments sound familiar?

"What do you mean, I have a drug problem? *You're* the one with the problem."

"You're so uptight all the time, maybe taking a drink once in a while would help you relax."

"I'm not an alcoholic. Alcoholics drink until they black out. I've never blacked out."

"Me? A drunk? Drunks get the DTs. Not me. I've never seen a pink elephant in my life."

"I'm not an alcoholic. I just like the taste of Scotch."

"Addicted? What a laugh. I can quit any time I want."

"I control the cocaine. The cocaine doesn't control me."

"I gotta party with my clients. If I didn't they'd find somebody else who would."

These remarks are typically heard from addicts. But denial is contagious. It can spread to *every* member of the family, as well as close friends, employers, and society as a whole.

Here are some remarks I've heard parents of addicted

children make: "Drugs are just a phase; all kids go through it." "Oh, Nora will grow out of it." "Jason is a sensitive child. We think it's better not to rock the boat." "In my parents' generation it was booze. In our day it was pot. Today it's cocaine. So what's the big deal?" Each of these comments, in its own way, is a form of denial.

Spouses of addicts have their own vocabulary of denial. "She promised she'd stop tomorrow, or next week, or after the first of the year, or when the pressure lets up at work." "Don't worry, I'm always there to make sure he doesn't have more than four drinks after dinner." "I buy the booze, so I always know how much there is in the house." "Look, he's doing less coke than before I married him. That's a step in the right direction." "She's under a lot of stress right now. Drugs make her feel better." "If she thought I had turned against her, there's no telling what she might do." By now you no doubt recognize not just denial, but the sounds of codependency and enabling, in remarks such as these.

Employers are good at denial. "I hire only good people; I'm too smart to hire a drug addict. I don't need a drug testing program in my business." Even when an employee falls apart on the job—missing deadlines, turning in shoddy work, calling in sick—employers often deny the signs of trouble.

Nor, as I mentioned earlier, are doctors immune. Some of them will deny the evidence of their own highly trained senses; they'll misread the lab reports or misinterpret the symptoms. Even if they do identify a problem of drug abuse, some of them may follow an inappropriate course of action. "My patient says he only uses drugs because he is under stress. I'll prescribe an antidepressant or an antianxiety drug. That should help. And it will be easier on me than trying to cure him of addiction." Granted, these doctors are usually motivated by compassion. Given the stigma that drug use has in this culture, doctors are very hesitant to label their patients as addicts because they know that long-term problems could ensue. But physicians who deny an obvious drug problem, even out of compassionate motives, are sweeping the problem under the rug and violating their sworn oath to "do no harm."

A person's choice to use drugs is in itself an act of denial. For one thing, our society has determined that drug use should not be permitted, and that choice is expressed in our laws that make drugs illegal. Drinking alcohol may be just as dangerous to one's health, but our society has decided—wrongly, perhaps—that alcohol poses an acceptable level of risk. But drug use is illegal. Period. Thus the choice to smoke pot or crack or to use any illicit drug is, by definition, an antisocial act. The user is denying our culture's collective judgment that drugs are unhealthy and dangerous.

In the last few years we've seen a complete turnaround in our cultural attitudes toward drugs. Before, they were tolerated. Cocaine users were looked on as "high rollers"; people who used hallucinogens were admired as "psychic pioneers" trying to expand the frontiers of consciousness. That's changing, thank goodness. Look at the ads that appear on TV, on buses, and on billboards: No longer do we tolerate drugs as funny, cool, or hip. Think about that public service message you've seen on TV, the one that shows an egg as a voice says, "This is your brain." The egg is cracked into a frying pan. As the egg sizzles away, the voice says, "This is your brain on drugs." Surveys have shown that such powerful messages have reached a lot of people and have helped to change their attitudes about drugs. Every day, the news-papers carry reports about the health hazards of drugs: crack lung, heart problems, threats to unborn children. The list, sadly, is endless.

My point is that people who still decide to use drugs today, despite the vast amount of antidrug infor-mation available in the various media, have to work very hard at building an immense wall of denial around themselves. They have to shut out loud and clear warning signals coming at them from every conceiva-ble direction in order to follow through on their urge to smoke, snort, or shoot drugs. If their friends and family abet them in their denial, it may be impossible to save them.

RATIONALIZATION

Rationalization—a cousin of denial—means twisting logic and common sense to suit one's own ends. When people rationalize, they invent self-serving but errone-ous reasons to account for their actions. In doing so they justify their destructive feelings, behavior, or motives that would otherwise be intolerable.

Drug use reinforces itself. Once drugs enter the body, they try to take over. Crack cocaine is especially powerful in this regard. So rapid is its action, so intense is the high that it produces, that it virtually comman-deers the pleasure centers of the brain. Cocaine causes the brain to release its entire supply of a chemical called dopamine, a neurotransmitter that signals nerve cells to fire and create sensations of pleasure. The problem is that cocaine doesn't bother to tell the cells to *stop* releas-ing dopamine. Eventually the cells deplete their entire supply. Now, usually the cells reabsorb the dopamine once it has done its job of activating the nerves. But coke blocks this reabsorption. Thus cocaine puts a double-whammy on the brain: It triggers the release of its supply of neurotransmitters, then prevents it from reusing that supply. Eventually the brain comes to depend on an outside source of chemicals to trigger the pleasure response, which is why cocaine is so addicting. That's why we say that drugs, especially cocaine, stimulate their own taking.

Once people are hooked, they have to keep justifying their actions. I've heard patients go to amazing lengths to rationalize why they keep using drugs, despite the impact on their family and their health.

Example: One patient told me he smoked crack because it made him "feel good." When I pointed out that he had been hospitalized twice for severe respiratory problems and depression, he said, "Yeah, that's the price I had to pay." This is what he meant by "feeling good"?

Another example: A patient, a creative director for an advertising agency, said she usually snorted coke three or four times during the course of the day. "It helped give me a creative edge," she declared. When I pointed out that she had been fired from her job because her recent campaigns had flopped, she said, "It was just politics. Some of the people there are jealous of my talent." That's rationalization.

OTHER DEFENSE MECHANISMS

Intellectualization is related to rationalization. When people intellectualize, they attempt to disguise their intense inner feelings and avoid examining their emotions by creating a smokescreen of "reasoning." Not long ago I treated a 23-year-old woman named Marina, who had been ordered into treatment by the courts after it was found that, due to her severe addiction, she had neglected the welfare of her 18-month-old baby. During our conversation Marina came out with some wild and frightening statements: "I didn't really neglect the baby, see, because I read somewhere that you shouldn't be an overprotective mother. If you give kids too much attention you'll hurt their development. See, kids have to learn early on not to be too dependent on their mothers, so really, I was doing what was best for her. You understand?" I understood—that she was intellectualizing.

Projection happens when people attribute their own thoughts, feelings, or desires to someone else. Fred, for example, was a master at manipulating the people around him into doing his bidding. Not only had he managed to con his sister into putting him up, rent-free, in her apartment, he also got her to agree to pay all the bills (and supply the drugs) until he could get a job—which, so far, had taken more than a year. Yet to hear him tell it, Fred was the victim, not the victimizer: "My sister practically begged me to stay with her. She was lonely, she said. So okay, I'll stay with you, I said. She won't accept any money from me—she does that just so she can hold it over my head. She's so manipulative— always has been, ever since we were babies." Fred was projecting his own worst qualities onto an innocent bystander so he wouldn't have to deal with his problems himself. Granted, his sister had a severe codependency problem of her own, but she was under the spell of a master Svengali.

Compensation, as its name suggests, occurs when a

person subconsciously tries to make up for some kind of failing, whether real or imagined. Jamie, for example, was a 25-year-old shipping clerk whose height was just under five and a half feet. Although he was by no means abnormally short, he began to feel that all of his problems— trouble finding a girlfriend, trouble keeping a job—were due to his stature. Through therapy Jamie discovered that he used drugs, in part at least, because as long as he stayed high he stopped having obsessive thoughts about his height.

Another example involved Mike, a boozing, coke-addicted "biker." While in therapy, he revealed that as a child he had been sexually molested. With time, he realized that his whole life had revolved around proving to the world that he was a "real man."

Splitting, a term often associated with borderline personality disorder, also describes the very common tendency of addicts to divide the world into all good or all bad. These people see the world in extremes—either something is right or it's wrong; good or bad—with no middle ground or balance. "If they aren't perfect, then they must be a failure." Therapy for these people involves the sometimes difficult process of helping them move beyond seeing the world as black or white to looking for the thousand shades of gray in their life and in the world.

There are about a dozen other clinically identifiable forms of defense mechanisms, but this is enough to give you an idea of what we are up against when we treat addicted patients and their codependent families.

THE CHALLENGE OF DUAL DIAGNOSIS

As a rule, the defense mechanisms and other psychological strategies drug users employ to protect themselves are products of the addiction itself. The pleasures of drugs are so intense, and the consequences of addiction so horrible, that addicts must twist reality into an unrecognizable form if they want to continue in their practices. In other words, the patterns of denial and psychological self-defense usually emerge *after* the person is caught in the clutches of a drug habit.

In many cases, though, some sort of mental disorder exists, not as a *result* of drug abuse but as a contributing *cause*. In other cases, patients have more than one medical or psychiatric condition at the same time. To describe such cases, we use the term dual diagnosis.

At Fair Oaks, we examine each patient carefully in order to rule out—or in—the possibility of some other concurrent disorder. Surprisingly, some physicians fail to take this simple step, and thus fail to find the clues that may lead them to a deeper understanding of their patient's condition. But study after study shows how crucial it is to look for some other problem that may be contributing to the patient's use of drugs.

For example, virtually half of the patients in a typical doctor's practice have significant medical and psychosocial problems associated with alcohol abuse. It's not uncommon for alcoholics to suffer from a panic or anxiety disorder. If an alcoholic stops drinking and a week later goes into a panic, many people would dismiss the problem, saying, "Poor Charlie—off the sauce for a few days and already in trouble." What's happening is not that Charlie needs a drink; instead, his new sobriety has allowed his underlying panic disorder to emerge. Charlie needs to be treated for this condition—a medication called imipramine usually does the job—or there's a risk that he'll start drinking again, feeling—wrongly— that booze is his only hope. There's no doubt that living without alcohol can cause an alcoholic to feel panicky for a while. But a careful doctor will distinguish between that *temporary* sense of panic and a coexisting *anxiety disorder*.

Reports indicate that 22 percent of patients admitted for the treatment of substance abuse also met the criteria for bipolar mood disorder (mood swings). Today we can identify several types of bipolar mood disorders. The most severe is known as Bipolar I, or what we used to call "manic depression." But the type I encounter most frequently is Bipolar II. Perry, whose story I told in Chapter 1, had a Bipolar II mood disorder. Although these people never really experience an extremely elevated mood, their normal, everyday level of energy is a notch above that of a normal person. These are the people who can hum along for 18 hours a day, seven days a week, and who can get by on a few hours' sleep a night. But we also find in these people a high rate of alcoholism and drug addiction, and because their moods can shift very quickly, they are at high risk of suicide. We've all heard of someone who, to all outward appearances, was successful and seemed happy and energetic, but one morning hanged himself, seemingly for no reason. As we saw in Perry's case, treatment with lithium helps smooth out the peaks and valleys for people with bipolar disorders.

Depression is another common part of a dual diagnosis. Some studies suggest that up to half of the cocaine addicts treated meet the criteria for major depression *after* they have been weaned from their drug. This suggests that in many cases, people who suffer from low mood are attempting to medicate themselves through the use of illicit drugs. Other patients have signs of attention-deficit hyperactivity disorder.

The chances of successful therapy improve if the doctor can identify all of the patient's specific problems and choose the right treatment for each of them. Fortunately, treatment for substance abuse often does a great deal to improve the patient's other psychiatric conditions.

As a rule of thumb, patients with a dual diagnosis must be treated for their substance abuse problem *first*. For many patients, especially women, addiction becomes their channel for expressing anger, sadness, or shame. Only when active substance abuse stops can we diagnose these other problems.

When, if ever, to use antidepressants for alcoholics with depression is still somewhat controversial. And, except during the detoxification process, alcoholics should not be given the tranquilizers known as benzodiazepines, since there is a high possibility that they will begin to abuse these drugs. One recent study showed that alcoholics tend to get euphoric on the tranquilizer alprazolam (Xanax), thereby increasing the risk of addiction. It appears that the brain cannot tell the difference between alcohol and Valium or Librium or any of the benzodiazepine medications. Whenever prescribing medication to the alcoholic or drug addict, I must always consider the potential for addiction.

Dual diagnosis patients and their families need to be educated about the two or more different illnesses they have, and must understand that each has to be treated separately and seriously. In most cases, freeing people from drug slavery results in great improvements, not just in their moods and their personalities, but in their whole outlook on life.

FAMILIES

One of the main goals of family therapy is to help the addict's loved ones recognize the defense mechanisms that contribute to the problem and that interfere with treatment. As you might imagine, a good deal of time is spent wrestling with the concept of denial. Fortunately, the very fact that the patient is in treatment means that a good deal of his or her denial has been overcome already. That means we can focus on the denial that may exist among family members—parents, spouses, children. In later chapters we'll talk specifically about techniques for overcoming denial.

Another crucial aspect of treatment involves educating the family about the other types of psychiatric illness that contribute to addiction. I try to explain to them that the situation is similar to having a relative who is confined to bed because of injuries resulting from a severe auto accident and who is also suffering from emotional problems because of that confinement. Physical therapy is needed to help mend the broken bones, while antidepressant therapy can help elevate the patient's mood. Similarly, treatment aimed at the substance abuse problem will help free the patient from addiction, while treatment aimed at an underlying psychiatric problem can help prevent relapse.

Another important lesson we communicate in family sessions is the invaluable role that self-help groups play in long-run recovery. If you've ever attended a meeting of AA, Al-Anon, or other such groups, you know that participants are highly aware of the many psychological ploys addicts use to rationalize or deny the extent of their illness. Should some members try to justify slipping back into use of drugs or alcohol, others in the group will point out the error of their ways in no uncertain terms. There is no substitute for this kind of long-term, day-to-day support when it comes to dealing with the psychological issues of addiction, but only if any underlying psychiatric condition is treated properly.

CHAPTER 4

THE BIOLOGY OF ADDICTION

As they sat in my office, Ken and his wife Trisha held each other's hand tightly. I asked what had motivated them to get treatment for Ken's drinking problem.

"Ken's father was an alcoholic," Trisha replied. "He died last year. His liver gave out. He was only fifty-two years old, but by the end he was a total wreck, emotionally and physically. His death was slow and painful. I think that scared Kenny."

"I am my father's child," Ken said. "I look like him, I sound like him—and I drink like him. But I don't want to die like him."

THE DISEASE MODEL

For decades, drug and alcohol addiction was seen as the result of a moral failure. People who had a problem with chemical dependency were viewed as being "weak" and "lacking in willpower." Typically they had to endure such comments as:

"Why don't you just stop hitting the bottle?"

"You know what your problem is—you have no self-control."

"Addicts are losers."

"You just can't face reality, so you escape by using drugs."

"Pull yourself together!"

"Snap out of it!"

How many times, in struggling with addiction in your family, have you heard remarks like these? For that matter, how many times have you made them yourself?

In helping families deal with addiction, I often ask them to take part in a little mind experiment. I tell the family we're going to reverse roles for a moment. I ask the spouse or parents of the addicted person to imagine that they have a chronic disease, such as diabetes. I remind them their condition requires that they watch their diet carefully, exercise regularly and rigorously, and give themselves insulin injections several times a day. If they fail to follow this regimen, they risk developing coronary disease or blindness, or falling into a coma.

Then I ask the person with the addiction to repeat some of the remarks he or she has heard. For example, during the experiment, the addicted patient might turn to her husband and say, "I'm tired of you being sick all the time. Why don't you just snap out of it?" The husband, assuming the character of a person with diabetes, replies, "How can I 'snap out of it'? I have a physical illness! That's like saying, 'Just snap out of a cold.'"

The dialogue continues: "If you had any amount of willpower, you could cure yourself." "That's nonsense. Willpower has nothing to do with this. All the willpower in the world won't help me as much as one injection of insulin."

It doesn't take long for the family to see the point of this exercise: *Addiction is a disease*. Like other diseases, it is a physical problem with physical and psychological consequences. When they see addiction in this light, families begin to understand the true nature of the problem they are confronting.

Thinking of addiction as a disease helps in many ways. For one thing, it underscores the fact that some people—perhaps as many as one out of ten—are born with a physical vulnerability to drugs. Something in the makeup of their bodies and brains puts them at higher risk of developing a problem with chemical dependency. For another, it keeps us aware that some people are more vulnerable to the effects of drugs once they enter the body. Further, the disease model allows us to identify the stages of the illness. Finally, and most important, it suggests which forms of intervention and treatment might be of most benefit.

THE CONTRIBUTION OF AA

The revolution in our thinking about addiction is due in large measure to the efforts of Alcoholics Anonymous. Founded in 1935 by Bill Wilson and Dr. Bob Smith—ordinary names for extraordinary men—AA now has two million members around the world. The AA philosophy is based on the idea that alcoholism is a physical problem, not a moral one. Through its no-

nonsense strategy, AA has improved and, in many cases, actually saved the lives of millions of people.

To benefit from AA, alcoholics must admit to themselves and to others that they lack the inner power to stay sober. They must recognize that, in a sense, they are permanently disabled—their addiction is incurable, and they are always at risk of relapse. Alcoholics are very often powerless to maintain sobriety under their own steam. Thus a sober alcoholic considers himself engaged in a lifelong struggle: always recovering, never recovered.

If the problem is seen as a lack of *inner* power to control the craving produced by physiological forces, then the solution lies in seeking help from *outside* sources. One source is spirituality; another is the love and support shown by fellow alcoholics during AA meetings. There is sobriety, as well as safety, in numbers. Unlike much of the outside world, the group accepts the alcoholic despite faults, foibles, and past behavior. Drinkers come to depend on fellow AA members, rather than on alcohol, to fill their emotional needs. Thus the pattern of compulsive substance abuse is replaced by communication, emotional closeness, shared experiences, spirituality, and the work of helping others regain their equilibrium. In AA, surrender is victory.

Many families are surprised to hear me, a psychiatrist, speak of Twelve-Step programs in such glowing terms. They had heard that AA and doctors are "at war" with each other. To a degree that is true; doctors want to cure their patients, while the Twelve-Step philosophy holds that no cure is possible. And some Twelve-Step groups oppose other forms of treatment, including the use of medications, on the grounds that one drug is just as bad as another.

True, there is no medical treatment for drug addiction per se—there is no pill that will cure a cocaine habit or a drinking problem. But many substance abusers do suffer from underlying psychiatric illnesses—the dual diagnosis patient I described in Chapter 3. These patients can benefit from the appropriate use of medications. Often when problems such as depression or mood swings are brought under control, the patient feels less of a need to abuse chemicals.

THE GENETIC BASIS OF ADDICTION

For more than half a century, researchers have been aware that alcoholics often report a history of alcoholism in their families. Since the 1970s, studies have shown that people with this so-called familial alcoholism have symptoms that are distinct from other types of alcoholics; their illness shows up earlier in life and is more severe. Depending on the criteria used, up to 55 percent of alcoholics entering treatment are found to have had an alcoholic parent. If you define alcoholism as a "major life problem with alcohol" and consider both first-degree relatives (parents, siblings) and second-degree relatives (aunts, uncles, and so on), then as many as 80 percent of alcoholics seeking treatment may be seen as having the familial form of the disorder.

As a rule, compared with other types of alcoholics, people with familial alcoholism begin drinking earlier in life, drink more alcohol each day, have more problems related to alcohol use, and seek treatment at a younger age. They are more likely to have problems such as truancy, antisocial behavior, trouble holding a job, and run-ins with the law. They suffer more blackouts and are less able to stop drinking once they start. Interestingly, some studies show that alcoholics with an alcoholic father tend to demonstrate a different pattern to their illness than those whose mothers were alcoholic. Furthermore, alcoholics whose close relatives have some form of major psychiatric disorder, such as depression, are more likely to develop a more severe drinking problem earlier in life than other types of alcoholics.

Of course, a child of alcoholic parents will grow up in a household fraught with tension, pain, and suffering. Some experts make the point that, given such an atmosphere, many people would grow up suffering severe psychological trauma that manifests itself as alcoholism. In other words, they argue that environment, not heredity, is to blame for the problem. As in all complex issues, I don't think we can state confidently that alcoholism, or other forms of chemical dependency for that matter, are the result of one factor and not the other. It's closer to the mark to say that *both* environment and heredity play a role to different degrees in different people.

What evidence do we have that substance abuse is hereditary? Several fascinating studies have tackled the problem by studying alcoholism in twins. One such study found that when one of a pair of identical twins (twins who share the same genetic structure) was an alcoholic, there was a six out of ten chance that the other twin would also develop the disease. In contrast, among fraternal twins (twins who don't share a genetic makeup), the odds were less than three out of ten.

Critics of such studies point out that the psychosocial problems that twins may face in growing up together may contribute to alcoholism. To weed out that factor, then, other research has been done on children who were born to alcoholic parents but who were adopted into different families. The findings indicate that adopted children whose biological parents were alcoholics still tend to develop alcoholism at a rate two or three times that of the general population, even when raised by adopted parents with no history of alcoholism. Conversely, children born to nonalcoholic parents but adopted into alcoholic families do not develop alcoholism at a rate greater than the general population.

Research shows that up to 70 percent of cocaine addicts have a family history of alcoholism. There is even evidence that some people have a genetically transmitted vulnerability to THC, the active ingredient in marijuana. For these people, smoking dope a few times can trigger addiction. At this point, however, we don't know how to identify these vulnerable people until they actually begin to use drugs—and of course, by then, it's too late.

In addition, a very recent report suggests that researchers may have isolated the gene responsible for transmitting a vulnerability to alcoholism. Such findings underscore the point that heredity is a major risk factor in the development of a substance abuse disorder. As with other medical and psychiatric problems, chemical dependency is best seen as a result of the interaction of biogenetic, psychosocial, and environmental factors.

THE BODY ELECTRIC

The process of becoming chemically dependent is a complex one. In a sense, it begins at the moment of conception, when the person-to-be inherits the family tendency to develop substance abuse or some other psychiatric illness. Other genetic traits may cause a person to have inadequate supplies of certain brain chemicals, such as neurotransmitters, which may contribute to the problem. Recent research has shown that, compared to men, women have a lower supply of the enzyme that breaks down alcohol in the body. Women are thus generally more susceptible to the effects of alcohol. As people grow and age, their medical history may also play a role: diseases that disrupt normal body functioning, surgery, chronic use of medications, and so on. And as we have seen in previous chapters, psychological and social factors also play a part.

In the past decade or so, our ability to study the living body has become incredibly refined, thanks in part to sophisticated machines that allow us to see inside the brain. We now have evidence suggesting that the part of the brain called the limbic system controls the body's response to drugs, and thus controls the development of addiction.

In evolutionary terms, the human limbic system is a very old part of the brain that closely resembles the limbic system found in other mammals. Part of the limbic contains nerve cells that arouse and modulate feelings ranging from joy and misery to love and hate. Other parts help our memory to function, while others help us perceive a sense of reward. "Reward" refers to the body's way of telling us that we've done something right. For example, the brain rewards us for eating (an activity that helps keep us alive) by making food a pleasurable experience.

Drugs work by changing the way the brain functions. Because it is involved in so many operations, the limbic system seems to be particularly sensitive to drugs. Some drugs work by triggering the reward response. The brain is tricked into thinking, Hey, cocaine makes me feel great! That drug must be necessary for my survival. Give me more! That's what I mean when I say that drugs stimulate their own use. To make matters worse, the limbic system records this pleasurable experience in its long-term memory banks. Under the right circumstances, then, the brain might think, Gee, remember how nice that drug made me feel? Maybe I'd better signal the body to get hold of some more.

Scientists refer to this cycle of use/reward/more use as "entrained" behavior. In time, such behavior can become as powerful as our drive to eat, drink, or have sex. That's why addiction can be difficult, if not impossible, to eradicate. It would be equivalent to trying to "cure" someone of appetite or thirst.

THE STAGES OF ADDICTION

The disease model—conceiving of addiction as a biological illness—allows us to trace the course of the illness, just as we trace the course of pneumonia or a common cold. It's clear that addicts pass through certain stages on their way to total chemical dependency. If we can recognize those stages, we can intervene sooner, provide appropriate treatment, and prevent the tragedy from getting worse.

The first stage is known as the "experimental" stage. This involves occasional, spontaneous use of beer or marijuana, usually at weekend parties among peers. Most people go through this phase as adolescents.

Passage into the next stage occurs when the person starts using the drug alone, often before going to school or work. This is when tolerance develops; someone who at first got plastered on two beers or wiped out on half a joint now needs more drug just to feel the same effect.

At the third stage, drug use takes over more of the person's time and energy. Solitary use becomes more frequent. The need for money to support the habit means that many users turn to dealing. Others steal from parents, employers, even friends. Many people who reach this point notice that drugs are beginning to interfere with their lives—they may get into trouble at school or with the law.

It isn't a very big leap to the final stage: dependency. At this point the person uses drugs daily, finding it very hard to skip a day. The physical side effects of the drug cause problems. Alcohol and drugs like cocaine squelch the desire to eat; many users become malnourished and suffer from vitamin deficiencies. Poor nutrition weakens the whole system, making it susceptible to diseases. Addicts who use needles to inject their drugs risk contracting life-threatening infections ranging from hepatitis to AIDS.

For people in this final stage, drugs become the whole focus of their lives. They form relationships only with other users or with dealers. Their only pleasurable activities revolve around drug use. In the early stages, people use drugs mostly to get a pleasurable buzz. Further along, however, they use them more to ward off the unpleasant feelings of "rebound" or withdrawal. Those who are cocaine-dependent, for example, admit they often snort coke not to feel good but to keep themselves from feeling bad.

Another trait of this stage, as we've seen, is denial. So many times I've looked into addicts' sunken, gloomy eyes and listened as they said, "Drugs are no problem for me. I'm in control."

To summarize these stages: Use leads to tolerance; tolerance to abuse; abuse to chemical dependency and addiction.

BIOLOGY IS NOT DESTINY

Some of you reading this book may be thinking, "Fine. My loved one's drug problem is inherited, it's hard-wired into the body. There's nothing we can do to root it out. Then why bother going into treatment?"

Whenever concerned family members make such comments, I reassure them: *Biology is not destiny*. Just because someone inherits a genetic predisposition does not *necessarily* mean that person will express that trait.

Think of it this way. You may come from a family in which every relative for the past three hundred years has been obese. But if you live on a desert island with almost nothing to eat, you will never become obese. You have the genetic tendency to be fat, but your environment will not allow you to express that trait. Similarly, people with the tendency to develop diabetes can often keep the disease at bay through careful diet and exercise.

That's why treatment is crucial, and that's why I see treatment as a form of education. We need to educate drug abusers and their families that biology, psychology, and sociology—the biopsychosocial elements I've described in these chapters—all interact to produce a problem with substance abuse. By being aware of their genetic heritage, and by working to control behavior and environment, people can do a great deal to prevent chemicals from taking control of their lives.

CHAPTER 5

WHEN INTERVENTION IS NECESSARY

Not long ago Nathaniel, a minister, came to see me. He wasn't looking for treatment for himself. Instead he was concerned because a dear friend and next-door neighbor, Woody, had a serious problem with alcohol.

"I've known about it for years," said Nathaniel. "I've even tried to talk to him, first as a friend and then as his minister. I guess I wasn't forceful enough, because the problem has continued, and it's gotten worse. Last week was the capper. Woody was driving home from the bar. Just before he reached his house he blacked out and plowed through my hedge. Fortunately he wasn't hurt. We managed to get him into bed. The next morning Woody was carrying out some garbage. He saw me in my yard and said, 'Hey, what happened to your hedge?' He honestly had no idea of what he had done.

"I've thought a lot about the problem. I've prayed a

lot, too. It occurred to me that perhaps Woody needs to talk to one of his peers. That's why I've come to you." Woody, you see, was a physician and quite well known in his community in southern Florida. We had met on a professional basis a number of times.

I suggested to Nathaniel that perhaps the time had come to stage an intervention. An intervention, I explained, is a strategy where people concerned about a substance abuser organize themselves and confront the person face-to-face. The goal is to break through the wall of denial and convince the addict that treatment is needed. Nathaniel agreed eagerly. "This," he said with a smile, "could be the answer to my prayers."

We drew up a list of people who should be present at the intervention: Woody's wife, his daughter, a partner in his medical practice, his golfing buddy, Nathaniel, myself and some others—ten in all. We met one evening to discuss and rehearse our approach.

On the day of the intervention, Nathaniel managed to convince Woody to join him for dinner. Before heading for the restaurant, though, Nathaniel said he had to stop by Fair Oaks Hospital for a short emergency visit with one of his parishioners. "Why don't you come in for a moment?" he said. Woody agreed. The reception- ist suggested they go to one of the hospital meeting rooms. Woody walked in—and there, seated in a circle, were nearly a dozen of the most important people in his life.

His face was the very picture of surprise. "What are you doing here?" he stammered. Nathaniel replied: "We're here because we all care very deeply about you. Sit down now. We have a lot of things to discuss."

OVERCOMING RESISTANCE

The word intervene means "to come between." That is precisely what happens in an intervention: People come between the addict and the addiction to break the cycle and begin the process of recovery. Intervention is a way to convince a chemically dependent person to accept help, even when that person doesn't want help or doesn't think there is a problem.

Intervention often takes place after people have tried every other means they can think of to help their addicted loved one—pleading, bargaining, threats, tears. The longer the addiction has lasted, however, the more entrenched it becomes and the harder it is to break it. The great thing about staging an intervention is that the family need not wait until the addict has "hit bottom," nor need they wait until the addict gets around to asking for help.

Interventions are so effective because they involve the elements of surprise, drama, and confrontation. When an addict, caught off guard, must face a roomful of people, each armed with incontrovertible evidence of the problem, there is virtually no escape. There is nowhere to go but up. According to dependency experts at the Betty Ford Clinic, intervention works in as many as 85 out of 100 cases.

Many of you reading this book have probably gone through some form of intervention already, whether you handled it yourself or worked in collaboration with a professional intervention counselor. If you tried intervention but it didn't succeed, perhaps this chapter will identify what went wrong and how to correct it. Other readers may be learning about intervention for the first time. For this group, I will try to spell out the steps to take and the pitfalls to avoid.

When I tell families about the strategies of intervention, many of them resist the idea. "It sounds so cruel" is one typical response. I assure them that, on the contrary, an intervention is an act of love, perhaps the most courageous act possible under the circumstances. The goal is not to punish, but to shatter the shell of denial addicts build around themselves. It takes a powerful weapon to break through a powerful defense. I explain to families that they won't be able to communicate their love until their addicted relative is prepared to receive their message. Intervention is a compelling way to accomplish that goal.

"But we have to lie and trick the person into showing up. How can we pretend we're trying to get the addict to face the truth when the whole process is based on deceit?" As a minister, Nathaniel wrestled with this troublesome issue. He found it very hard to mislead his friend, even though it was for his own good. I tried to reassure him, as I reassure other families, that in a sense we are not lying to the patient. Instead we are trying to distract the "guards"—the psychological defense mechanisms—that have imprisoned the patient behind a wall of denial. We are rescuing the patient and must sometimes use cunning, and a little bit of force, to do so.

"If we confront Joel [or Jane], we'll just make him [or her] angry. He [or she] will claim it was all a set-up and we'll lose the battle." During a confrontation patients often do get angry, and there is some risk that the anger will be so great that the intervention will fail. More often than not, though, the patient isn't the only one who is angry. Parents, spouses, children, friends, employers can be angry, too—angry that drugs or alcohol are ruining their relationships with the person in the hot seat. The challenge is to express that anger in a positive and healthy way, and make sure that expressions of love overshadow feelings of anger.

One last point before we discuss the intervention process itself. Many times families resist staging an intervention because they themselves have become dependent on having a sick relative to care for. If the addict gets better, they will no longer be able to use the addiction to distract themselves from their own problems. They will have to redefine their roles in life. The spouse who has been a martyr to the mate's chemical dependency no longer has a cause to be devoted to. Adult children who abandoned their careers or have turned down offers of marriage because they felt they had to take care of their sick parents must now deal with a frightening new reality. These codependents must be shown that intervention will help free them from their own prisons as well.

THE INTERVENTION PROCESS

If you are ready to try intervention, I strongly urge you to work with trained professionals. True, some families who take the "do-it-yourself" approach succeed in getting their loved one into treatment. But intervention is a delicate matter that touches some pretty raw emotional nerves. If mishandled, it can backfire. The addict might storm out of the room and refuse to have anything more to do with those who participated in what is seen as a "mass character assassination."

However, when a skilled counselor works with the
family to prepare them for the intervention, rehearse
their presentation, and manage the intervention itself,
then the chances of success are very high. Professionals
know the strategies that work and are trained to handle
the tears, the denial, the resistance that will emerge
during the session.

How can you locate people to help with the intervention? You might start by looking in the Yellow Pages
under "Alcoholism Information." Calling a local hospital
that specializes in the treatment of substance abuse will
connect you to a network of physicians, nurses, social
workers, and professional counselors who are themselves
recovering alcoholics. Your local AA chapter will have
some good suggestions for you. You could also ask your
family physician or a member of the clergy. Another
source is the National Council on Alcoholism in New
York City, whose toll-free number is 1-800-622-2255.

Caution: Before selecting an interventionist, be sure
you ask about the person's credentials in this field. A
well-meaning doctor or family friend who has no experience in managing an intervention might end up doing
more harm than good.

Merely confronting someone about addiction isn't
enough. The goal of intervention is to get the substance
abuser into some kind of treatment program. You must
therefore do your homework and check out the programs
available in your area *before* the intervention happens.
As we'll see in the next chapters, you have a number of
options. Some hospitals specialize exclusively in substance abuse; other hospitals have units devoted to treating
chemical dependency. There are outpatient programs
where people spend most of the day attending therapy
and counseling sessions but continue living at home.

You will need to decide which route you will take. Everyone involved must agree with the decision, so that you present the patient with a united front. One more thing: any treatment program you consider seriously must advocate participation in some kind of Twelve-Step program. If it doesn't, keep looking.

Another key element in your preparation is to educate yourselves as much as possible about the disease of addiction. Read everything you can get your hands on about the substance of abuse involved, whether it is alcohol, cocaine, marijuana, or some other drug. Hard truth is a powerful tool for chipping away at the wall of denial, and people present at the intervention must be equipped with the facts. See the reading list at the back of this book for sources of information about drugs and addiction.

Intervention is not a spontaneous event. It must be carefully planned for. You must therefore be prepared to have everyone involved meet at least once, and preferably twice, to discuss your strategy and rehearse your presentations.

One thing you must agree on is the need for surprise. If the patient gets wind of what you are up to, you may be unable to corner the person. Even if the patient does show up, he or she may have had time to prepare a "counteroffensive" strategy to thwart your efforts.

You need to decide who will be involved in the confrontation. There is no minimum or maximum number of people who have to be present in order for the intervention to work; too many can be unwieldy while too few may lack sufficient impact. The important thing is that you cover every angle of the patient's life. Here are some people whom you should consider inviting to take part:

The family: Of course, those closest to the addicted person must participate if the intervention is to be of any value at all. The spouse or significant other is probably the most important person when it comes to confronting an adult substance abuser, followed by the children and the parents. But don't overlook the value of having a special member of the extended family take part. A devoted sister, a cherished aunt, or a loving cousin may be the one to turn the patient around. Earlier we saw how it was the grandfather who persisted in helping his grandson. Keep in mind that anyone whose life has been directly and negatively affected by the patient's addiction should be invited to take part.

The employer: Don't overlook the impact that the patient's boss can have. Remember that economic pressure can be a powerful weapon. A patient who is told to clean up his act or he will lose his job is usually willing to accept treatment. In addition, the patient's supervisor or coworkers might be valuable sources of evidence about the impact of drug use on the patient's job performance.

The doctor: Fortunately, more and more physicians today share the view that addiction is a disease. They are sensitive to the physical impact that drugs have on the body and can tell the patient, in no uncertain terms, the type and extent of damage addiction can cause and can spell out the inevitable consequences. The best physicians are also alert to the types of treatment available and know which ones have the greatest likelihood of succeeding. Before inviting your doctor, however, be sure you discuss the subject carefully. If you find that you don't agree about the nature of addiction and its threat to your loved one, then it's best if that doctor were not involved.

Friends: Many addicts who tune out their family will listen when a friend speaks. And many of a substance abuser's friends are able to present evidence of the problem that no one else can. "Remember how we went bowling one night and you were so plastered you couldn't even let go of the ball?" "Remember how you were so excited about seeing your favorite rock group in concert that you paid a scalper $200 for tickets, then got so blasted on drugs that you freaked out and spent the entire time in the medical emergency tent?" Caution, though: Friends are friends because they are loyal to one another. I've seen more than one intervention ruined because the friend refuses to "gang up" on his buddy. As with any possible participant, be sure and screen everyone thoroughly before letting them take part.

Acquaintances: I know of interventions where the patient's lawyer or insurance representative has taken part. These people can offer hard facts about the impact of addiction on the patient's life: legal consequences, financial burdens, and so on. Sometimes a policeman or a judge can be an imposing presence. In one case the patient's most important client was present to say he would withdraw his account unless the patient got help. Young people may be especially responsive if an important teacher or athletic coach takes part.

Where should the intervention take place? There are several alternatives. You might consider a friend's house, a church, an office conference room, a hospital, or a community facility. It may even be all right to conduct the procedure in the patient's own house or apartment, although it may be harder to arrange it. You should be aware that the patient's natural inclination will be to bolt and run. If you do the intervention in the patient's own home, it's easier for that person to flee to the bedroom or bathroom and lock the door. Should that occur, don't do anything to restrain the patient or force the patient to return to the scene.

We've discussed the cast of characters and the setting. What is the script you should follow? The details are subject to negotiation, but here are some guidelines.

The first thing each participant must be prepared to do is state clearly that they are acting out of loving concern. I encourage everyone involved to write out a statement that goes something like this: "Mom, I love you and I am very concerned about your drinking." You should take turns reading these statements. During the rehearsal for the intervention, others may wish to offer suggestions on how to improve your message. That's fine, but make sure that what you say is what you feel. And do plan to write these thoughts down and read them out loud. Better not to improvise, since you may get carried away by your emotions. Whatever the words, the love has to shine through. WARNING: The patient may willfully ignore you, or scoff at you. "You don't love me! If you did, you'd leave me alone." Be prepared to let such remarks roll off your back. Stay focused on the fact that you have the patient's best interests at heart.

During the next phase, participants take turns recounting examples of how the addict's behavior affected them personally. A son might say, "Dad, I was totally humiliated last month when I had a party in the family room and you stumbled in drunk and started dancing with my girlfriend." The boss might say, "John, I was looking for the financial report on your desk one night and I found a nearly empty whiskey bottle in your drawer. Now I know why you've called in sick nearly two dozen times this year." In Woody's case, Nathaniel described how he plowed through the hedge but didn't even remember the event the following morning. The goal of this phase is to present the addict with *clear, incontrovertible evidence* of the problem. This evidence must be so strong and so dramatic that it is absolutely impossible for the patient to deny, defend, or dismiss it.

The next phase is in many ways the hardest. Each participant must state what he or she will do if the patient refuses to go into treatment. In other words, the people present must state the *consequences* that will result. These consequences are not punishments, not idle threats. They are firm, clear warnings of what will happen if the situation doesn't change.

In one recent intervention, a son told his mother that if she persisted in her drinking he would not allow her to babysit or otherwise be alone with her grandchildren. "I can't trust you to be responsible for their safety if I know you are still drinking," he said. "What if they get hurt or need a doctor? How will you be able to drive them to the emergency room?" In another case, a father told his daughter that unless she got off cocaine, he would cut off all financial support: he would stop paying for her college, stop making payments on her car, and would even alter the terms of his will. A friend might vow never to bail the patient out of jail again. An employer can say that without treatment, the patient will be out of a job. One of the most powerful consequences possible is when the spouse threatens to walk out of the marriage unless the patient agrees to get help.

The key to success is to *make absolutely certain that participants only state consequences that they are prepared to carry out.* Substance abusers are pretty sharp:

They know when people are trying to, excuse the expression, bullshit them. A wife who says she will seek a divorce but doesn't mean it has no power over the addict. The goal is to force the drug user to realize how serious the situation is, and what will be lost if he doesn't go into treatment. Idle threats are useless. Clear consequences that will have a serious impact on the addict's life are a powerful weapon, perhaps the most powerful of all.

In many interventions participants tell the addict, "We are serious about this. We have enrolled you in a treatment program at XYZ Hospital. The hospital is waiting to admit you right now, tonight. We have packed a suitcase for you and a car is outside waiting. We love you and want you to begin treatment this very hour. If you do not, the consequences we have described will be put into effect as of this moment. What is your choice?"

If the intervention has been handled properly, there is no choice. The addict, taken by surprise, is confronted with firm evidence of his problem. His nose has been rubbed in the mess he's made of his life, and he has no room to maneuver. There is no escape. He can't say, "I'll go to my friends; they understand"—because those friends are there in the room with him. He can't say, "My wife or my parents will protect me"—because they're sitting there as well.

The wall of denial has come tumbling down.

One last point: Regardless of the outcome of your intervention, it is possible that some of the family members involved will need some kind of followup support. They will have been through a rough time indeed. Not only have they had to confront their substance-abusing loved one, they have had to confront their own fears and emotions. They have had to reassess their lives and their relationships with the chemically dependent person. Some of them have been stripped of their identity as a codependent and may need help building up a new and healthier identity. Thus, whether or not the addict chooses to enter treatment, other people involved in the intervention may realize *they* need some kind of therapy or counseling.

CHAPTER 6

FAMILY SUPPORT IN
THE INPATIENT SETTING

If, through a staged intervention or some other means, you have managed to get your addicted relative to accept treatment, you have my congratulations.

But don't rest on your laurels yet. The battle is barely half over. Yes, of course, the addicted person needs treatment—but so does the entire family. Here's an odd fact about therapy for addiction: If the substance abuser is to recover fully, the family must also get help. What's more, the family can recover from codependency *even if the addict refuses to get treatment.*

Why should this be so? Remember what we have learned thus far about the family and its contribution to addiction. To some extent, the risk of chemical dependency is biological in origin. Families may need to be educated about the risk of inheriting a vulnerability to alcohol and drugs. Even if they have never abused substances themselves, parents or spouses may think or act in ways that can trigger substance abuse in other family members and that may reinforce the pattern of abuse once it has begun.

In many cases the patient's addiction has become the focus for all of the family's dealings with one another. This might mean that both married partners use the husband's alcoholism to distract themselves from their deep-seated animosity toward each other. Parents may devote themselves to managing their daughter's cocaine addiction as a way of shutting out their feelings of failure or unhappiness. Take away the addiction and suddenly these families are faced with a new and possibly overwhelming set of problems to be solved.

Family therapy works on several levels: First, it teaches the facts about drugs and addiction. Second, it makes families aware of their harmful patterns of behaving and communicating. Third, it teaches them how to break those patterns and replace them with new and healthier means of interacting. Finally, it helps reinforce the family structure when the "glue" that has held it together—the patient's addiction—has been dissolved.

The fact that you are reading this book is a sign that you are serious about getting help. What's more, you have (I hope) accepted the fact that you, and others in your family, will have to take an active part in treatment if you truly want your addicted loved one to get better.

I want now to describe the process of family therapy—how it is structured, who is involved, what happens, and why. In this chapter I will focus on family therapy that takes place while the patient with the addiction—also known as the "identified patient," or IP—is undergoing treatment in the hospital or in some other facility. In the following chapter we will see how families can get help even if the IP refuses treatment, and how therapy must continue for months, even years, in order to support the patient and prevent relapse.

SHOPPING FOR TREATMENT

If you have staged an intervention, then you may have already decided which treatment plan in your area is right for you. If you are still in the planning stages or are shopping around for a program, let me point out a few things you should be aware of to help you make the right choice.

As I've said, addiction is a combination of biological, psychological, and social factors. *Each* of these factors must be addressed in treatment. Unfortunately, experts don't yet agree on exactly which form of treatment works best. Addiction isn't like mild pneumonia; doctors don't observe the patient's symptoms, prescribe some medicine, and send the patient home. Instead, caregivers must assess the situation carefully to spot problems and devise solutions. Sometimes the caregiver may focus on one aspect of the problem and ignore the others. For example, psychologists will concentrate on the behavioral side of things, but are not able to conduct physical examinations and prescribe medications that may relieve underlying problems, such as depression, that may be contributing to the addiction. Similarly, a physician may work to repair the physical damage caused by substance abuse, but may ignore the problems at home that triggered the patient's addiction in the first place.

That's why I strongly urge you to choose a treatment program that uses a team approach. At my hospital, for example, our staff includes physicians, social workers, and psychologists, as well as counselors who are themselves recovering alcoholics. Such a structure covers just about all the bases. And of course, any program worth its salt must pay particular attention to the needs of the family. Of course, whole families will benefit by attending counseling sessions. Often, too, these families gain invaluable support and insight when they attend multifamily sessions. In these sessions a dozen or more families meet and share their stories of love, hope, and survival.

Another thing you should determine is whether the therapy program adjusts to fit your special needs. Programs that attempt to treat all patients and their families in exactly the same way are useless. There are too many variables—patient age, level of development or maturity, the type of substance abused, family problems—to expect a cookie-cutter, one-size-fits-all approach to be of much value.

One more thing: You must feel comfortable with your caregivers' "bedside manners." This is an abstract quality, and is hard to measure or define. You may find yourself disagreeing with your doctor's basic philosophy or techniques, or feel that you simply don't like the doctor's style. I encourage you to respect your own feelings and keep shopping. You don't have to be intimidated just because the physician has a wall full of diplomas and certificates. If you find yourself in an adversarial position with the treatment staff, then you'll just be wasting everybody's time and money and you won't achieve your basic goal, which is to help your addicted relative get better.

ELEMENTS OF EFFECTIVE THERAPY

As I mentioned, there is no real consensus on which kind of treatment is best. However, there are four definite phases involved in any family therapy program.

Any program you are considering should state clearly from the outset that *abstinence from drugs or alcohol is the first goal*. Thus the first phase calls for patients and their families to develop a system that will achieve abstinence and then—this is the tricky part—maintain abstinence over time.

In order to develop such a system, family treatment begins by assessing the nature of the problem and the impact it has had, not just on the IP but on the whole family. Your caregivers will need to know how much drug use there is, what kind of drugs are used, how long the problem has existed, whether there is a family history of drug abuse, and so on. In many cases this assessment takes place with the IP and the family present in the same room. Such a discussion may be the first time the family has ever talked about the problem face to face, and often produces a surprising amount of honesty and confession. What's more, with two or more people present, a more complete and balanced picture of the problem often emerges. When a concerned and caring physician or other treatment professional is present, this initial interview works to lay the important groundwork for the therapy to follow.

The assessment helps determine what the best strategy will be for achieving abstinence. If the patient is an adolescent living at home, and the level of drug abuse is mild or the addiction hasn't been going on for a long time, then it may be possible to handle the problem on an outpatient basis. If the patient is somewhat older and the problem is moderate, but has not progressed to outright chemical dependency, then outpatient care and participation in a Twelve-Step program might do the trick. However, if drug use has severely disrupted the patient's life, and if the level of dependency is high, if the patient refuses any kind of self-help approach, or if the level of addiction requires medically supervised detoxification, then hospitalization is usually needed to achieve abstinence. Some addictions, especially to crack cocaine, may be so powerfully entrenched that hospitalization may be necessary to break the cycle of drug binges.

It's natural for a family to resist hospitalizing an addicted relative. There's a lot of fear and mistrust; sometimes, unfortunately, our society attaches a stigma to people who have sought help for psychiatric problems. Fortunately, that situation is changing. Nowadays it's more often the people who *don't* get help when they need it who are stigmatized.

Hospitalization has many advantages when dealing with a deeply rooted problem like addiction. For one thing, it provides a controlled environment where we can monitor patients 24 hours a day as we support their struggle to remain drug-free. A hospital with a caring staff of people with different types of expertise allows patients to get the kind of help they need when they need it. Being in a new situation, away from home, where every minute of their time is structured and they have no access to illicit drugs shows patients how to change their behavior to lessen the risk of relapse. If the hospital is on the cutting edge of addiction treatment, caregivers will know the latest and most effective strategies for dealing with drug cravings and for managing symptoms of withdrawal. Many families find it a great relief to have their addicted relative removed from the home for a while and put into the hands of people who understand their struggle and their pain. The dramatic step of hospitalizing a troubled family member, in itself, helps calm the family's agitation, allowing them to shift their focus from the problem and to begin concentrating on the solution.

Nevertheless, even if the patient—or the family—refuses to accept hospital care, there are still many treatment options open, as we'll see in the next chapter.

Once the family has agreed on the need for hospitalization, the second phase is to *determine a strategy for family therapy.* This phase might start when the family seeks advice on how to conduct an intervention, such as I described in the previous chapter. In other cases it means overcoming the family's resistance to treatment by educating them about the problems of codependency and enabling. Fortunately, I find that most families will agree to come in for at least one initial visit. Once that door has been opened, I try to show that not only am I concerned about their situation but I know of ways that will help relieve their suffering. During our first conversation they usually realize that by resisting family treatment they are, in effect, saying that they want the patient's problem to continue.

A family is more than just the people who live together in one household. For my purposes, a family also includes any relatives from different generations who have contact with the identified patient once a week or more. Ideally each of these people will attend a therapy session at least once during the course of treatment. In reality, we must often settle for less—just the spouse, or just one parent, or one parent and a sibling or child. Part of the process of determining our strategy is to figure out which family members are absolutely essential to the process, and concentrate on motivating that group of people to take an active part in treatment.

The third phase is *the actual process of family therapy itself,* which I'll describe in the next section. Once that step is completed, the final phase involves *helping the family make adjustments in their lives once the patient has stopped being a substance abuser.* Remember that many families have made the addiction the focus of their psychic and physical energies. Once that "center of gravity" has been removed, families need to rediscover how to interact with each other in new and more loving ways.

THE THERAPEUTIC PROCESS

In dealing with a family, the treatment team needs to examine the ways the individual members interact and communicate. Which members have formed alliances; which members oppose each other? What roles do the members play in the family? Are those roles rigidly defined and are they appropriate for each person's level of maturity? Does the identified patient play one parent off another, for example? How does the family handle conflict and resolve crises? Do the members act as mindreaders, guessing at what each other is thinking or feeling, and base their own actions on such guesses? How do the members fight among themselves?

Answers to these questions are necessary in order to identify, and then treat, unhealthy patterns of interaction. Obviously, unless we caregivers set up hidden cameras or become flies on the wall, we can't watch the family in its home. We must bring them into the hospital and observe them as they interact. In doing so we can make a more accurate diagnosis about the true nature of the family problem.

Next, the treatment team decides which strategies are likely to be of most help. For example, one method works by using therapeutic sessions to show the family how to substitute new ways of interacting for their old destructive and repetitive cycles. During these sessions the therapist becomes, in a sense, a temporary member of the family whose role is to guide the process of change. Another method concentrates more on the disturbed thought patterns that family members might have developed over the years.

One method I find particularly helpful concentrates on showing families how to change their behavior to minimize conditions that lead the IP to become substance dependent. We educate families about the types of interactions that enable drug abuse to exist and continue. We explain how drug use can be triggered by certain stimuli; as one patient told us, "Whenever my children start screaming at each other, I just have to have a drink." We then work on ways that the family can avoid or change these triggers. Another goal is to show the family how to offer positive reinforcement to the recovering addict. We work with the IP to recognize harmful thought patterns—self-derogatory remarks ("I'm no good") or feelings of guilt—and replace them with more accurate and rational ways of thinking. We help the family and patient plan alternative actions in response to the urge to use drugs—going for walks, taking in a movie. Through role-playing we help families rehearse their reactions to problems they typically encounter. Toward the end of the program we review the therapeutic process and reinforce the new skills that the family and the IP have learned.

Regardless of the method used, the goal is to help family members learn how to communicate with each other. Sometimes they have trouble even recognizing their own feelings, let alone expressing them. We try to show that it's *okay* to be afraid, it's *okay* to be angry. Just as important, we try to show that when you do feel angry or tense, there are ways to express those feelings that don't involve relying on drugs or alcohol.

Often families have lost their ability to communicate not just feelings but thoughts as well. In one case the husband tried to explain something that had happened at work but made a grammatical error. His better-educated wife pounced on the mistake, gloating in triumph. The husband clammed up, left the table, and went on a three-day drinking binge. We worked with that couple to help the wife become more tolerant of such errors and to help the husband become less sensitive to criticism.

We also stress the importance of nonverbal communication. Sometimes families forget how actions speak louder than words. Recently I handled a case where the husband said he told his wife three times a day that he loves her—but on the night of their anniversary, he went bowling with his buddies. Sad and lonely, the wife went to a friend's apartment and spent the whole evening smoking crack. The husband was sending his wife mixed signals. We underscore the need to let our actions match our words, and encourage families to express their warm feelings toward each other both verbally and nonverbally.

In our program at Fair Oaks we offer patients and families a number of ways to avail themselves of family therapy. Our social workers have the primary responsibility for interacting with families and helping structure the program to suit their needs. In my capacity as physician I work mainly with the patients themselves, and conduct weekly individual sessions and daily group therapy sessions with them. Many times an issue will emerge in these sessions that has an impact on the family. In those cases, or when I have been asked to do so by the social worker or the family, I will take part in a family therapy session. By being present I can steer the conversation around to some of the important problems that have emerged and still do so without violating the patient's right to privacy. I can also offer a medical perspective, explaining the physical effects of drug abuse or educating the family about the therapeutic process.

Another key element in the program is multifamily therapy. On Thursday nights we invite parents, spouses, adult children—any family member who wishes to attend— to join with the IP in a group session. During these meetings, which are conducted by a team of two social workers, families have a chance to air their thoughts and feelings. There is no agenda for those sessions; patients and loved ones alike are free to bring up and explore any issue that is of concern to them at that moment.

When they first hear about such sessions, many family members resist the idea of taking part. "I'm so ashamed that my father is a drunk," said one 34-year-old woman. "How can I sit in a room full of strangers and talk about how hurt and angry I am?" I tried to explain that she would be with a group of people who already understand what she is going through and who would be extremely sympathetic to her pain. Many of them have been dealing with similar problems for much longer than she has, and may have some helpful things to say to her.

It was gratifying to speak with this woman after the session and hear that, indeed, she felt much better. "I was able to say things in front of strangers that I've never told even my closest friends," she reported. "Somehow being in a room of caring and supportive people made it possible for me to tell my father things to his face that I never could before." I replied that during the session she was exposed to some of the most powerful and healing words in the English language: *"I know how you feel."* I also emphasized that, once her father was discharged, they would both benefit from ongoing participation in a Twelve-Step program (AA for him, Al-Anon for her) where the same loving support could be found every day of the week.

Every hospital's program has a different structure. Some may not offer multifamily therapy, but will concentrate instead on the needs of an individual family. At Fair Oaks we recently inaugurated a program on Saturday afternoons where families and patients are invited to come and discuss specific topics. (The multifamily sessions, in contrast, do not focus on a particular theme that has been decided upon in advance.) These Saturday sessions are led by a rotating team made up of social workers, psychologists, and recovering substance abusers. Over the course of a typical four- to six-week program, then, patients and families are able to discuss a range of issues. These sessions, which are completely voluntary, underscore our philosophy that treatment for substance abuse is largely a process of education and communication.

THE FINAL PHASE

During the period of hospitalization, both the patient and the family focus their energies on the immediate problem of substance abuse. They learn the facts about addiction, discover the faulty thinking and behavior that reinforces the pattern, and find out about ways to change those patterns. By working individually and collectively, family members learn about themselves and their addicted loved one and train themselves to act as a team to defeat their common enemy.

But in a sense, the time spent in the hospital is like boot camp—intensive training in survival skills. The true challenge comes when the patient is discharged from the hospital to face the real world again. Suddenly the patient must leave an isolated environment and return to the home, the job, the old friends, the old haunts. The risk is that reentering that world will trigger the urge to abuse substances once again. As I've said, the process of recovery—and the risk of relapse—is a lifetime concern. Thus, as important as hospitalization may be, the period of time following discharge is just as critical.

In looking for treatment, be sure that the program includes some kind of aftercare. At Fair Oaks, patients who have graduated from therapy—our "alumni"—may attend free group therapy sessions twice a week for up to two years after discharge. Further, the patient and one other family member (a parent or significant other) may also attend one other weekly session for up to two years. These sessions are run by addiction counselors who have themselves triumphed over drugs or alcohol. They thus offer participants the benefit of years of personal experience in fighting the temptations of drug use one day at a time.

As valuable as these sessions are, I am frankly shocked at how few alumni take advantage of them. I think that's a reflection of how difficult addiction is to

eradicate. It also shows how, despite completing a four-
or six-week course of hospitalization, many patients just
aren't ready to accept the need for support in their
struggle to recover and remain abstinent. For that reason, we strongly advocate that both patients and families take part in a Twelve-Step program. In the next
chapter we'll discuss how the philosophy behind such
programs serves as a cornerstone for the lifelong process
of overcoming addiction.

CHAPTER 7

FAMILY SUPPORT
OUTSIDE THE HOSPITAL

Not long ago I spoke to a group of people who were struggling with addiction in their families. A woman asked me where the best drug treatment facility in the country was located. I replied, "What is your address?" She told me, and I said, "*That's* the best place."

My point was that treatment has the best chance of succeeding when the addict and the family work together to reinforce at home the lessons learned in the hospital.

The goal of inpatient care is to prepare patients for their return to a normal life. By definition there is no "normal" life inside the hospital. Once discharged, the recovering substance abuser may be faced with many of the same challenges as before: a circle of friends who may still use drugs; a routine or dissatisfying job; tensions between others in the household. At best, inpatient therapy teaches ways of responding to these challenges without resorting to chemicals. When the family has also been taught how to use these tools and how to communicate better among themselves, the chances of avoiding relapse and breaking the cycle of codependency and enabling increase enormously.

Family members need not handle the lifelong process of recovery on their own. As we'll see in this chapter, the options for ongoing help and support—for the patient as well as the family—are many and varied. This help is available whether or not the patient undergoes a period of hospital treatment. However, if these approaches are to work, the family must understand what they are about and must participate in them as actively and fully as possible. Further, even if their addicted loved one drops out of treatment, family members must realize that they can continue to benefit from counseling and support, whether in individual therapy or a Twelve-Step program, for as long as they feel the need.

With that in mind, let's discuss some of the many options available to you.

TYPES OF OUTPATIENT CARE

Ideally, every person struggling with dependency would be treated as an outpatient. That may surprise you, coming from a physician whose entire practice is based in a hospital. But it's true. Why? For many reasons. Outpatient treatment can be just as effective as hospitalization—if the patient is motivated to work at getting better and if the substance abuse is not associated with medical or psychiatric problems that require hospital treatment. Outpatient care costs less and is generally more widely available. There is less of a stigma attached to it and it is less disruptive to the patient's life.

One type of program is an *outpatient clinic* affiliated with a hospital. These clinics provide counseling and support for people and their families who are trying to kick their habits while they continue to live and function within their community. Such clinics provide access to medical staff and other hospital-type services needed to address the physical and psychiatric aspects of addiction.

Methadone maintenance programs, in theory, help people addicted to heroin make the transition to a drug-free state. Addicts visit the clinic to receive a dose of methadone, a synthetic heroin substitute. Ideally, patients receive lower and lower doses until they no longer need any drug at all. Unfortunately, methadone maintenance levels often are not tapered—but are continued at the same maintenance levels. If at all possible, I do not recommend this course of treatment.

Residential therapeutic communities are highly structured programs lasting as long as 18 to 24 months. Substance abusers live together and work to change the habits and attitudes that fuel their drug problems. They must obey strict rules and participate in intensive workshops and group therapy sessions. Examples of residential programs include Village South (in Miami), Phoenix House, and DAYTOP Village.

Halfway houses are, as their name suggests, steppingstones in the transition from hospital care to drug-free living. They are short-term residential communities where recovering addicts can live with others who understand their concerns until they feel ready to return to their own homes and families.

Twelve-Step programs such as Alcoholics Anonymous are essential for long-term recovery. I'll discuss these programs in a moment.

CHARACTERISTICS OF GOOD OUTPATIENT PROGRAMS

Whatever course you follow, make sure the program is one that advocates complete abstinence from all drugs. Surprisingly, some programs say it's okay for patients to use drugs occasionally. I disagree, and so do most addiction experts. Not long ago I treated a man for cocaine abuse. He did very well in therapy and was drug- and alcohol-free for two years. One night at a party he decided to celebrate his success by having "just one beer." After all, alcohol wasn't his problem, coke was. But one beer wasn't enough; he had to have another. Within a short time he had downed a whole six-pack. His inhibitions thus lowered, he accepted a snort of cocaine when it came his way. Bang—he was hooked all over again. A month of treatment, two years of sobriety, went out the window. That's why we advise all of our patients that they must never use any form of drugs or alcohol again, ever. That's a tough order to follow, but it is necessary.

Programs should also educate patients and families using the latest information about the hazards of drugs. Some caregivers base their treatments on out-of-date notions. The worst example I can think of is the physician who still claims that cocaine is not addicting. Every day new evidence arrives showing the dangers of drugs. Recently, for example, "crack lung" made the news—a symptom of smoking crack cocaine that in-

cludes severe chest pains, violent coughing, and other
horrors. If you sense that a treatment program hasn't
kept pace with modern research into drugs and addiction, keep shopping.

Good treatment programs encourage patients and
families to change but don't resort to lectures or ha-
rangues to do so. A positive attitude is important. Also,
check to make sure the program is targeted to the
patient's age, interests, and special needs. Because
their problems and concerns are so radically different,
young marijuana abusers and elderly alcoholics, for
example, should probably not be placed in the same
therapy group. By the same token, patients and families often find that joining a group that concentrates
on marital issues or parent-child conflicts is more
effective.

Of course, for a program to be worthwhile it must
involve parents, spouses, or other people important in
the patient's life. Some programs concentrate exclusively
on the abusers themselves, which conveys a subtle—and
wrong—message that recovery is a private matter that
doesn't involve anyone else.

The most effective programs use regular drug testing
to monitor compliance. Ideally, patients should be asked
to give urine samples two or three times a week. Some
people object to this strategy, claiming that drug testing
invades privacy and reflects a lack of trust. In my view,
the opposite is true. Many of my patients give in their
urine sample reluctantly but understand that it helps
them stay honest. Drugs cause users to lie and deny
their problem to themselves and to others; urine testing
eliminates the self-deceit that so often sabotages treatment. What's more, knowing that they will be tested
helps because it enables patients to control their urge to

use drugs. Often recovering patients remark, "I wanted to smoke some pot at a party last weekend, but I was able to hold out because I knew I had to come in for a 'whiz quiz' on Tuesday."

THE PHASES OF TREATMENT

A good outpatient program is one that realizes addiction and recovery both occur in stages and that offers support at each of those stages. Patients who have graduated from hospital care have already learned much of what they need to know. For them, outpatient treatment is a way to review the key points, to consolidate what they know, and continue to work on recovery. Patients who have not been hospitalized, however, may be hearing this information for the first time. The program should make sure that these "first-timers" understand what is happening to them.

The first phase is abstinence. Treatment should concentrate on making patients drug-free and keeping them that way for a month. To reach that goal, a patient may need to see a therapist daily for counseling and support. Family members may also need guidance frequently during this time, especially if they need help themselves in eliminating their own use of drugs or alcohol.

Once drug use is under control, patients enter the next phase, which involves working to identify the things that trigger their drug urges and ways to control and eliminate cravings. Drug use is largely a conditioned response. Just as cigarette smokers often crave tobacco after eating, for example, a crack smoker who always did drugs in a dark room may feel the need to light up whenever someone draws the curtains or dims the lights. At some point, the treatment program might involve helping the patient return to the real world—old hangouts and so on—to gauge how powerful these triggers are and how strongly the patient can resist them. Family support is vital at this stage, since members may need to learn how their behavior and attitudes can be the trigger that stimulates the patient's drug abuse.

Following abstinence, and once cravings are under control, work begins on the need to anticipate and prevent relapse. A program that claims it can "cure" addiction and thus eliminate the risk of slipping back is lying to you. Denying that relapse can occur means there is no contingency plan for dealing with it when it does. A patient who is prepared for relapse and has a strategy to cope with it is much better off than the one who succumbs to an urge, smokes some cocaine or takes a drink, and says, "Well, I've blown it. I'm a failure."

The final phase is known as consolidation. Typically this phase arrives about a year after treatment begins and continues indefinitely. Consolidation means that patients have been taught the facts and they know which strategies work for them and which don't. Patients may join new therapy groups that focus on the long-term challenges of living a drug-free life. Sometimes during this phase recovering addicts struggle with overconfidence—"Hey, I've been clean for a year, I don't have to worry any more." In other cases people whose use of drugs has covered up some underlying psychiatric problem discover that, since drug use has stopped, the symptoms of their other disorder are beginning to emerge.

Typically, during the consolidation phase, family

members begin to think, "Well, we've done all we can to help Dad (or Junior). He's on his own now. We can't dwell on his drug problem any more. We have to get on with our own lives." Such feelings are understandable. The struggle to overcome addiction can be relentless and exhausting. Nonetheless, I urge families at this stage to renew their efforts to helping the patient remain drug-free. They may need to remind themselves how to act so as to avoid triggering the patient's drug urges. They may want to make a commitment to attending more family-oriented Twelve-Step meetings. Importantly, they should review their plan of action for dealing with the patient's relapse if it occurs.

THE TWELVE-STEP APPROACH

For many years there was a near-state of war between the medical profession and the people who advocated a self-help strategy for dealing with chemical dependency. In one camp were the doctors. Psychiatrists, for example, tried to uncover the psychological motivations that drove a person to drink. Other physicians believed that their patients drank because they were depressed and so they prescribed antidepressant medications that attacked the symptom but not the cause. In the other camp were those who felt that alcoholism was a disease, not a moral weakness, and grew angry that doctors and other respected members of society refused to understand that reality.

While the battle is not quite over, the two camps have reached a pretty solid truce. Within the last few decades physicians have by and large come to view chemical dependency as a physical disease with psychological complications. By approaching the problem from a medical point of view, we have been able to discover new and better techniques for treating the illness. Many physicians have also recognized the therapeutic value attached to the spiritual aspects of the Twelve Step philosophy. At the same time, the Twelve Step movement has shown itself considerably more willing to accept that some substance abusers do indeed have some form of underlying medical problem, which may respond to treatment with medications or psychotherapy. Both sides have learned from each other, and the world is better off for it.

"Twelve-Step programs" is a generic term referring to any self-help groups who model themselves after Alcoholics Anonymous. AA created a list of a dozen steps that must be taken during the process of recovery (see Box on page 93). So solid, so valid is that philosophy that it applies to basically any situation where a person wants to be free of a slavish addiction—whether to a substance, another person, or a pattern of thought. In recent years we have seen the rise of Cocaine Anonymous, Narcotics Anonymous, and Overeaters Anonymous—even Gamblers Anonymous.

AA was intended for people who themselves had a problem with alcohol. But the families of alcoholics were also suffering from the pain of addiction's impact on their lives. As a result, they banded together to form a companion group known as Al-Anon. Another spinoff, targeted for children of alcoholics, emerged as Alateen. Other Twelve-Step groups followed suit, until today we have Coc-Anon, Nar-Anon, and a number of other variations.

Each of these free programs is run by volunteers

THE TWELVE STEPS OF ALCOHOLICS ANONYMOUS*

1. We admitted that we were powerless over alcohol—that our lives had become unmanageable.
2. Came to believe that a Power greater than ourselves could restore us to sanity.
3. Made a decision to turn our will and our lives over to the care and direction of God as we understood Him.
4. Made a searching and fearless moral inventory of ourselves.
5. Admitted to God, to ourselves, and to another human being the exact nature of our wrongs.
6. Were entirely ready to have God remove all those defects of character.
7. Humbly asked Him to remove our shortcomings.
8. Made a list of all persons we had harmed, and became willing to make amends to them all.
9. Made direct amends to such people wherever possible, except when to do so would injure them or others.
10. Continued to take personal inventory and when we were wrong promptly admitted it.
11. Sought through prayer and meditation to improve our conscious contact with God as we understood Him, praying only for knowledge of His will for us and the power to carry that out.
12. Having had a spiritual awakening as the result of these steps, we tried to carry this message to alcoholics, and to practice these principles in all our affairs.

*Reprinted with permission.

who are themselves recovering from substance abuse. These people are further along on the road to recovery from dependency or codependency, and thus offer positive role models for those whose struggle is just beginning. In these groups people are free to express their thoughts and feelings without fear of being judged or ridiculed.

There is great psychological benefit in simply getting these things off your chest. Sometimes, too, hearing someone else's troubles helps you keep your own in perspective. Ideally, members learn from one another how to solve certain problems or how to think in less destructive ways. By hearing "war stories," shyer or newer members might feel freer to open up and relate some of their own experiences. Simply knowing that other people are in the same boat—"I know how you feel"—can be a tremendous relief.

If you want to help your loved one overcome addiction, perhaps the single most important step you can take is to join a Twelve-Step program in your area. Remember, too, that each group develops its own unique identity. If you don't feel comfortable in one program, try to find another. Even if your addicted relative refuses treatment of any kind, you and your family will benefit from taking part in these sessions as often as you can manage.

A FAMILY AFFAIR

Much of the therapy I've described is aimed primarily at the identified patient. Of course, other members of the family must be aware of what their loved one is going through if they want to help the addict recover.

Even so, there may come a time when the process of recovery seems to grind to a halt. Either the patient or a family member refuses to do anything more about the problem.

For example, Chuck, one of my patients, came to see me a year after he was discharged from Fair Oaks. He said he had attended a lot of aftercare sessions and was active in AA. He had managed to stay sober the whole time. "The trouble comes when I have to visit my folks. My dad *always* has a beer in his hand. I can handle seeing him drink. I can handle hearing him slurp it down. *But I can't handle the smell.* As soon as I walk into the house, boom—I know there's a can of brew open somewhere. I gotta tell you, that makes me pretty thirsty. Sometimes it gets so bad I have to leave the house. Pretty soon I know I won't be able to visit them at all."

We decided to invite Chuck's parents to the next family aftercare session at Fair Oaks. During that meeting he found the courage to tell his father what was troubling him. After a thoughtful moment, the father said, "I didn't realize how sensitive your nose was. I see what you mean now about how the drug can take over your mind. I'll make you a promise: You call to let us know when you're coming over, and we'll make sure the booze is out of sight and we won't have anything to drink while you're around. I guess we can do without drinking if it means we'll get a visit from you."

A DRY HOME

Every family in recovery must address the question of whether or not to allow the presence of any alcoholic or mood-altering substances in the home. I strongly urge my patients to remove all mood-altering substances, including alcohol, from the home. This advice can be difficult for many family members to accept. I've heard more than one spouse say: "Just because she has a problem, I don't see why I have to give up my glass of wine with dinner." Fortunately most family members, when they understand the nature of addiction and the necessity of abstinence to their loved ones, realize the importance of a "dry" home. If a family member persists in keeping alcohol or any mood-altering substances in the home, then two points must be considered: (1) the family member also suffers from a substance abuse problem; or (2) the family member's commitment to, even love for, the person in recovery is suspect. In either case, the recovering person must not allow his recovery to be jeopardized; additional family counseling or substance abuse treatment for the other family member is strongly recommended.

In the previous paragraph I stressed that all mood-altering substances including alcohol should be removed from the home. The phrase "mood-altering substances" refers not only to cocaine and marijuana (which of course, must also be removed from the house) but also to a wide range of prescription and over-the-counter medications which can be mood-altering substances. In fact, many people are surprised to learn that a wide range of cold and allergy medications should be avoided (see the box on page 97.) Before taking any medication, I suggest that you discuss the matter with your physician or pharmacist.

As I've noted previously, drug use can mask other types of problems, including problems with relationships. Let me tell you about Anne, who was stuck in an unhappy marriage to Lew. She snorted cocaine to relieve

THE COMMON COLD

The common cold and hay fever pose special problems for people in recovery since a wide range of cold, cough and allergy products—both prescription and non-prescription—contain alcohol, codeine, or other potentially addicting ingredients such as hydrocodone bitartrate and hydromorphone hydrochloride that should be avoided by all recovering addicts. For example, the prescription medication Tussar-2 Cough Syrup contains codeine and alcohol (7 percent of the syrup), while the over-the-counter Nyquil Nighttime Colds Medicine is 25 percent alcohol! Read the ingredients list carefully. I recommend that all preparations containing either alcohol, codeine, hydrocodone or hydromorphone compounds be banned from the house.

This does not condemn the recovering person to a life of constant sneezing and sniveling, however. There are numerous medications, such as Actifed, Alka-Seltzer Plus Cold Medicine, Chlor-Trimeton, and Dristan Advanced Formula Tablets, that can be taken safely. Although most of these medications contain an antihistamine (such as chlorpheniramine maleate or diphenydramine maleate) and/or a decongestant (for example, phenylephrine) that can cause drowsiness, jitteriness, or a "spacey" feeling, these side effects, if they occur, are usually minor and short-lived. As a general rule-of-thumb, take these medications on an "as-needed" basis and start with their lowest effective dose.

her misery, she thought, but discovered that the drug was only making things worse. She managed to kick her habit; her coke-induced fog dissipated but her marital troubles didn't. Lew attended a few counseling sessions with her but soon dropped out. Eventually Anne mustered her courage and sought a divorce. As she put it, "Now I'm drug-free and Lew-free." It's possible that, had Lew been more motivated, therapy might have helped this couple resolve their differences.

Here's a contrasting example. Recently I treated a 36-year-old man for a cocaine habit. Martin was a particularly difficult case. He had been committed to the hospital against his will, he resisted attending group therapy sessions, and when he did attend he was disruptive, to put it mildly. I was professionally disappointed (though personally relieved) when he signed himself out of the hospital one day and vanished. However, his wife and two adolescent children continued to attend meetings of Nar-Anon, the support group for relatives of cocaine addicts. When I last spoke with them, they reported that they had overcome their anger and hostility at Martin, and were closer as a family than they had ever been when he was around.

There's a common thread that runs through the stories I've just told. Chuck came very close to telling his parents he couldn't be with them any more. Anne was forced to leave her husband for her own good. Martin's family found they were better off without him. Each of these people discovered that, in order to preserve their sanity, they had to let go.

Often a family will cling to an addicted member because they think if they give up they will be unable to survive the onslaught of guilty feelings. A mother will become addicted to her addicted son, refusing to release him into the hands of professional caregivers, and end up ruining her life. A husband will stand by his alcoholic wife out of loyalty, but in the process might alienate their children, ruin his business, and cut himself off from his friends. In each of these cases, the sorrow would be less if the addict or the codependent would just *let go*.

Perhaps the idea of giving up on a problem—or on a person—shocks you. "How can you tell me to just let go?" a woman asked me once. "I love my husband, and if I can save him from this horrible nightmare, I will. I won't give up trying till I'm dead and gone." I did my best to convey to this woman that if we have tried everything we could but the addiction persisted, then she was indeed at risk of dying an early and unnecessary death. I explained that drowning people often pull their rescuers under water, resulting in two corpses on the beach. The best lifeguards are the ones who know when to give up trying to save someone who will do nothing to save himself.

The wisdom of the strategy of letting go was driven home to me recently. A clergyman told me he had struggled with his daughter's drug use for years and had tried everything he could think of to help. Finally, one morning, he prayed for strength and forgiveness, and then threw his daughter out of the house, barely giving her time to pack a bag. The girl caught a train and went to stay with an aunt. During the next nine months she joined Narcotics Anonymous, weaned herself from drugs, found work, and pretty much turned her life around.

Last Christmas she surprised her father with a visit. She thanked him for what he had done. "You taught me an important lesson," she said. "When you let me go, I realized I had to let go of my addiction."

CHAPTER 8

WORKING TOGETHER TO PREVENT RELAPSE

Addiction is a chronic illness with no cure. That's one of the most important lessons families of substance abusers must learn. As I've explained, some people are born with bodies that crave drugs or alcohol. Once these substances enter the body, they cause physical changes in the cells of the brain and other tissues. These changes reinforce the craving, which leads to more drug use, and so on in a vicious cycle. No matter what type of treatment the patient has had, no matter how willingly the patient has complied with the program, the desire to use drugs again lurks just below the surface, ready to erupt when circumstances allow.

That's why any worthwhile therapy, whether delivered in the hospital or through a self-help group, must train patients and their families to *anticipate relapse*. Equally important, therapy must show how to *deal with relapse* when it strikes.

Actually, as a physician, I can see a positive side to the problem of relapse, or "slipping," in the vocabulary of AA. Think about it for a moment. If you have an infectious disease, such as pneumonia, you will exhibit a set of symptoms—fever, chills, cough, and so on. When medical professionals observe those symptoms and conduct tests, they can identify the cause of the illness and prescribe treatment. In addiction, relapse and the events that trigger it work the same way. They are symptoms that allow the patient and the caregivers to explore the problem areas and decide how to fix them. If, for example, an alcoholic finds he succumbs to the urge to drink whenever he attends a family gathering, then his therapists need to help him discover ways of handling pressure in those situations.

Another "advantage" of slipping is that it helps break through the wall of denial. Many addicts think they can control their problem. You know how it goes: "Just one drink." "No more than one joint a night." But for addicts, one drink or one joint is never enough. When they go on a binge and wind up in jail for driving under the influence or for possession of an illegal substance, they may begin to realize just how serious the problem really is.

Here's a key point to keep in mind: A relapse is not a sudden event. It is a process that unfolds over time. If you can spot the warning signs that a relapse is on its way, you can confront the addict. The more aware you are, and the earlier you act, the better your chances of preventing disaster.

Of course, if as a codependent you are in denial yourself, then you have a much lower chance of spotting an imminent slip. Perhaps at some point you've said to yourself, Oh, Jack just had a drink because he's been working so hard. When the pressure lets up, he'll get back on the wagon. By now you recognize such remarks as denial. That's another reason why families must take part in therapy. They have to overcome their own denial so they can anticipate and cope with relapse.

DANGER! RELAPSE APPROACHING!

What are the warning signs of relapse? Each chemically dependent person will exhibit his or her own pattern. It usually takes some time before the family can recognize that pattern. Nonetheless, in my years of working with addicted patients, I've noticed some consistent trends that warn of an impending slip.

One key trend is what AA refers to as HALT—an acronym that stands for "hungry, angry, lonely, tired." If a substance abuser becomes any one of these, the Relapse Risk level goes up.

Hunger. As I've said, drugs seize control of the body, redirecting the energy that should go toward normal, healthy activities and using it to force the person to seek more drug. In severe cocaine addiction, particularly among crack smokers, cocaine replaces the urge to eat. Likewise, in alcoholism, booze supplies the body with so many calories that the cells end up deriving the energy they need from booze alone. Of course, alcohol lacks the protein, vitamins, and minerals and other nutrients needed to maintain health. That's why so many alcoholics neglect their diet and suffer severe malnutrition. If you notice that your addicted relative is starting to skip meals or shows a change in eating habits, be on your guard. Addicts are prone to transform hunger pangs into drug urges.

Anger. Substance abusers tend to be highly emotional people to begin with. As we've seen, in many cases addiction reflects a person's efforts to self-medicate and relieve feelings of depression or smooth out the peaks and valleys. Anger is a blend of frustration and hatred. When the addict is overwhelmed by these feelings, the temptation to relieve them by resorting to drugs or alcohol is great. You and your therapist should discuss specific ways to handle and release anger without the use of chemicals.

Loneliness. This is an especially serious danger signal. We humans are biologically programmed to associate with one another. It's bad for both our physical and mental health to be cut off from other people. For addicts, the problem is worse. I've stated frequently in this book that group support is an essential part of recovery. When a dependent person drops out of his group of friends and stops taking pleasure in his former activities, the risk is great that he will turn to his old "friends"—booze and drugs—for comfort.

Tiredness. Battling addiction is a drawn-out and exhausting process, for dependents and codependents alike. And none of us is perfect. When we are worn down we make mistakes and errors in judgment. Such mistakes can put an addict in the hospital. Being tired may also cause the addict's family to ignore signs of trouble or fail to take the appropriate action.

Overconfidence. Graduating from therapy and staying clean for a period of time is a real boost to the ego. Addiction is such a formidable foe that people who have found the strength to overcome it feel powerful—and justifiably so. What's more, once they've flushed the chemicals from their bodies and brains, addicts feel healthier than they have in perhaps years. All of these factors may lead to overconfidence. A crack smoker, for example, may feel it's all right to go to parties where drugs will be used because "Now I know I can resist them." Maybe she's right. But it's not worth the risk to find out.

Magical thinking. This term refers to the way some people confuse cause and effect. They believe that just by thinking about something they can make it happen. Similarly, they may believe that by performing a certain "ritual" in just the right way, they can produce some magical effect. For example, an addict might say to himself, "If I can walk from the bus stop to my front door in exactly 644 steps, I know I won't have a drink tonight." You can see the problem immediately: If the alcoholic takes 648 steps to reach home that day, then he may think, "Well, I've blown it. Where's the bottle?" Another problem is that the addict's rituals may turn into some form of compulsive behavior that comes to dominate his life and the lives of his family. Lastly, magical thinking may cause addicts to believe that quack cures—Chinese herbs, dietary supplements, and the like— may solve their problem. Learn to identify these types of thoughts, in yourself and in your addicted relative, and banish them from your minds.

Castles in the clouds. All of us have big dreams for ourselves once in a while. For a recovering addict, those dreams may provide their motivation to get better. The thought process goes something like this: "Now that I'm off drugs, I'll have a lot of extra money to spend. This is the time for me to start that business I've always wanted to run. I'll patent that idea I had for a new Super-Widget—I'll sell millions of them! I'll make a fortune and retire in ten years!" The trouble is that such dreams take a lot of hard work (not to mention a healthy influx of capital). Disappointments, frustrations, and failures are likely. For the recovering substance abuser, such setbacks can trigger a relapse. As a codependent, you have a tough challenge: You must encourage thoughts and actions that could lead to a better life for both of you, but you also have to help your loved one deal with setbacks without resorting to a chemical crutch.

Self-pity. Anyone stricken with an illness is tempted to look up into the heavens and moan, "Why me?" Addiction is no different. Of course it hurts an alcoholic to see that other people can have an occasional drink without causing a problem. And when drug users find their family and friends have ganged up to pressure them into treatment, they may think—wrongly—"Nobody loves me, everyone's against me, no one understands." Likewise, as a codependent you may feel as if your entire life has been taken over by this illness. You are probably eager for your addicted relative to get better so you can tend to your own needs. Perhaps you've said to yourself or other people, "I can't take it, this is too hard, I can't go on, I'm so tired of this." Be careful: Self-pity is a sign of trouble ahead. Many substance abusers will talk themselves into such a low opinion of themselves that resorting to drugs or alcohol is the only option they feel is left open to them.

Crusading. This refers to the behavior of the recovering addict who suddenly makes it a mission to spread the word about sobriety or drug-free living. This is the person who goes up to someone having a drink at a party and says, "Well, I've been sober now for six months. Isn't it about time *you* did something about your drinking problem?" In some respects, there's nothing wrong with a little crusading. A kind word to a friend at the right time might mean one less addict in the world.

In its extreme form, however, crusading may mean a relapse is imminent. Why? Addicts may feel shaky or uncomfortable about their ability to stay clean. If they see people around them drinking or drugging, it may erode their fragile sense of self-confidence. Also, as I've mentioned, self-pity may creep in. Addicts may resent others who can use alcohol or drugs in moderation and not suffer life-threatening consequences. Rather than express their resentment directly, they transform it into a mask of virtue. Their "crusade" is really an effort to convince themselves to stay clean. It takes a lot of energy to keep up that front. When they stop to rest, a relapse may set in.

"Drug pushing." This is the flip side of a crusade. We see this behavior in the recovering addict who pushes booze or drugs onto family and friends: "Hi! Come on in! Have a drink. I can't join you, of course, but don't let that stop you. Have a good time!" It isn't hard to see that the addict may be creating circumstances that make a relapse inevitable. You've probably heard the excuses: "Well, everyone else was drinking. I'm trying to stay sober, but with the sight and smell of liquor everywhere, it's impossible to hold out!" In our treatment program we advocate complete abstinence. In many cases this means abstaining from even handling drugs or alcohol or, if necessary, staying away from places and events where these substances are available. Otherwise the temptation to relapse may be overwhelming.

Lack of discipline. In a very real sense, addiction therapy is a form of training. Patients learn how to think, feel, and act in ways to prevent drug use. This means making a commitment to staying drug-free—one day at a time, even one *hour* at a time. Trouble is brewing when the recovering addict suddenly forgets how important a sense of structure is. For example, the addict's sleep patterns may change—he may start staying up later at night. Or she may begin skipping work more frequently or dropping out of classes at the local junior college. Another warning sign is that the addict forgets to keep appointments or is late for them. It's especially troubling when the recovering substance abuser quits showing up for aftercare therapy sessions or Twelve-Step meetings. Typically, the addict might say, "I don't need that any more. I'm okay now. I can't stand being in a room full of losers whining about their problems. I can make it on my own." If you observe changes in your addicted relative's daily routines, keep alert for relapse.

WORKING THE PROGRAM

Knowing the warning signs of relapse is invaluable. Forewarned, as they say, is forearmed. But it's equally vital that you know how to help your addicted loved one recover from a relapse. You must be aware, too, that there may come a point where there is nothing you can do to help. At that point you may have to simply let go, as we discussed in the previous chapter. Fortunately, there's a lot that can be done before things reach that crisis stage.

The most important thing to remember is that *relapse is only a temporary setback*. It does not mean that treatment was a failure, or that the patient is a failure. In fact, if a therapy program is any good at all, it will teach you and your addicted loved one that relapse is virtually inevitable. The trick is to minimize the damage and by doing so strengthen those areas of weakness that the relapse reveals.

Another key to surviving this difficult time is to remember the importance of communicating with each other. The goal of family therapy is to teach members to open up and let others know how they're thinking and feeling. This can be tough. Changing the habits that have become ingrained in a 20-year marriage or that have existed in a family since the children, now adolescents, were born doesn't happen overnight.

Recently I talked with Rudy, a 44-year-old cocaine addict who had stayed clean since graduating from the Fair Oaks program 18 months earlier. He told me that, for several weeks now, he had been having intense dreams about cocaine. "If Walt Disney had developed a place called 'Coke World,' this would have been it," Rudy said. "In the dream coke is everywhere, falling out of the sky like snow. People go into restaurants and order trays full of the stuff. I'm there watching everybody getting high and at first I think it's pretty funny. But as the dream goes on I start thinking, Gee, I'm a little hungry myself. Maybe I should go into a restaurant and have something. Each time I have the dream I get a little closer to using the stuff. I wake up feeling a really strong urge to snort a couple of lines. Well, last week I did."

Coke dreams are not uncommon among addicts. The difference for Rudy was how he handled them. During family therapy, he made an agreement with wife Lucille that he would discuss his thoughts and feelings about his problem as openly as possible. In return she agreed not to criticize or condemn him for anything he said or did.

"We've worked out a kind of code," said Rudy. "I might come into the kitchen or call her from work and say, 'It's getting colder.' That's my way of saying that I'm starting to feel an urge to use drugs. At that moment, if it's at all possible, she'll drop whatever she's doing and give me her full attention. She usually starts by saying, 'How cold is it?' And I'll tell her what's on my mind. Lately we talk a lot about my coke dreams. She's been very supportive. She doesn't roll her eyes or say that she's tired of hearing about it. Instead she listens, she asks questions. She kind of 'talks me down' and will keep at it until I feel the urge isn't so powerful. After I slipped we talked about it. Instead of being angry she said she was proud of me for trying so hard and for keeping clean for so long. She said that we would just have to try even harder from now on."

Rudy and Lucille learned how to establish a channel of communication and keep the line open. Because he knew he could talk with her without fear of being judged or condemned, Rudy knows he is more able to keep his drug urges at bay. Imagine if the opposite were the case: Rudy comes down to express his fears about his dreams, and Lucille snaps, "Shut up! I am so sick of hearing about your dreams! If you are so desperate to get hooked on that stuff again that you dream about it all the time, why don't you just go ahead and do it and quit bothering everyone!"

Rudy's wife is obviously a caring and concerned woman. But she will admit there are times when she has troubles of her own and may be less patient with her husband. At those moments she will remind Rudy that there are a lot of other people who might help him. She is referring to their local branch of Cocaine Anonymous. ↑dy says he goes to CA meetings three or four times a ↑h and finds it of enormous value.

↑t's another part of working the program of recovery: linking up with an appropriate self-help group and staying with it.

One of the key elements of Twelve-Step programs is the concept of the sponsor. A sponsor is a person, further along in recovery, who agrees to work closely with a substance abuser to provide special counseling and guidance. Members of the group are encouraged to talk to each other after a meeting, find a sponsor, and exchange phone numbers. Then, whenever the urge to relapse strikes, the person can call the sponsor for help in getting through the crisis. It's not always easy to establish such a relationship; a member might feel shy or unworthy or reluctant to impose on another person. It may be hard, too, to place such an enormous degree of trust in someone who is probably a total stranger. But it's definitely worth doing. And codependents also appreciate knowing that there is someone available who might have more knowledge of what the addict is going through who can back them up in times of trouble.

Should a relapse occur it would be worth the time to review the list of the things that trigger the recovering addict's drug urges. Perhaps something has been overlooked that everyone needs to be reminded of. Similarly, if the addict has devised a list of alternative actions to take instead of using drugs—going to a movie, taking a walk or a cold shower—perhaps this would be a good time to find that list and discuss it.

A relapse often leads to severe feelings of guilt and self-loathing. It may be necessary to return to the treatment facility for a consultation with the therapist or to rejoin a therapy group. Family members may also want to "reenlist" in order to express their feelings of frustration and anger.

One relapse is no cause for alarm. In fact, it may be

a good way to measure progress—"One drinking binge in three years. Not bad, Mom! I'll bet you can go even longer this time!" However, if relapses recur with increasing frequency then action is called for. Remember how part of an intervention involved presenting the dependent person with a list of consequences that would befall if treatment was refused. Well, after the second or perhaps third relapse it may be time to invoke those consequences again. You may want to consider staging a "refresher intervention" where the family and perhaps some of the other original participants remind the addict what will happen if substance abuse persists. Having to go through that scene again is often enough to jog the person's memory and reinforce their desire to stay clean.

At this time, as before, people must be willing to put their words into action. That is, if the dependent person refuses to cooperate, the others must put the consequences into effect. This may be the point at which the codependents decide they have to let go—for the addict's sake as well as their own. My belief, however, is that with all the help available for today's substance abuser— professional counseling, therapy groups, self-help sessions— things seldom need reach this point of no return.

CHAPTER 9

SPECIAL NEEDS IN FAMILY THERAPY

As I write this book there are 18 patients undergoing treatment for substance abuse under my care. That means my staff and I are dealing with 18 family situations. Each case is different; each has its own set of circumstances that we must take into account. Let me give you an idea of the range of issues that come up.

At one extreme is Janice, a 27-year-old word processor who is seeking to free herself from her twin addictions to crack cocaine and alcohol. Janice says her family lives in another part of the country and has no idea either that she is an addict or that she is in treatment. She says that her father, a prominent state politician, "would have a heart attack" if he knew. Janice feels it is not possible to include her family in any aspect of her treatment.

On the other end of the spectrum is Vincent, 30

years old, who works in a furniture assembly plant. Vincent is married and has an infant son. He sought treatment for his cocaine habit after his wife Lynn threatened to leave him for good. Because she is concerned for her own welfare, as well as her child's, Lynn has taken an active role in the program, attending virtually every family therapy session available to her. She is very open and direct in her comments, expressing clearly how she feels about Vincent's problem and his efforts to get better. It is clear by the way these two interact during group discussions that they love each other very much. Because of that love, and their love for their child, they have made great progress together.

Most patients fall somewhere between these two extremes. Gary, a 25-year-old alcoholic, was into the third week of a four-week program before he convinced his mother to attend a multi-family session. His father, also an alcoholic, refused flatly to join her. During the session Gary found the courage to tell his mother that he loved her but resented the ways that she permitted him and his father to continue drinking. "I've learned a lot about codependency since I came here," Gary said. "You need to learn about that, too." Clearly his mother felt pain at hearing such things, but she said she would try to understand and to change her ways.

There are others: Mick, a 19-year-old who lives with his parents and who abuses marijuana and psychedelic drugs; Francis, a 56-year-old alcoholic divorced from his third wife; Celia, a 40-year-old Jamaican woman whose husband—also an addict—disappeared after the birth of their third child.

My point is that each of my patients comes from a different background and presents a unique set of circumstances. For families to benefit from therapy, the program must recognize these differences and work with them. To ignore them is to overlook what may turn out to be a key piece in the puzzle of addiction.

FACTORS AFFECTING THE COURSE OF THERAPY

By definition, family therapy means taking the needs of at least one other person into account. This person might be a parent, a spouse, a lover or significant other, a young child, an adult child, a sibling, a grandparent, and so on. A good treatment program is one that reaches out to these others and seeks to include them to the greatest extent possible. The broader the therapeutic support a program gives patients, the greater the chances that they can avoid relapse once they return to the "real world."

To an extent, the program should also take into account the patient's substance of abuse. Alcoholics may experience different feelings and problems than a co-caine abuser, for example. In reality, though, the specific substance involved is of relatively less concern than the biopsychosocial factors that cause and reinforce the addiction.

Another element is extent and severity of substance abuse—how long has the problem gone on, what stage has it reached, and to what degree has the patient's life been affected? What psychological or psychiatric symptoms have emerged as a result—constant trouble with the law, for example, or difficulty holding a job? What role does ethnicity, cultural heritage, or religious background play? How does the family react to each other—

do the members hide their feelings, do they try to read each other's minds, or are they overly sensitive? What channels of communication exist that can be used to overcome the problem, and which need to be established or reinforced? Another important question that some treatment programs may overlook is that of gender. What problems confront female addicts in today's society, and how do they differ from those issues that a male addict must handle? What are the special needs of pregnant or elderly addicts?

Let's discuss these issues in more detail. My purpose in doing so is to remind you that in shopping for treatment, you must feel confident that the caregivers will be sensitive to your family's specific needs and will work with your particular circumstances.

SUBSTANCE OF ABUSE

The patient's choice of drugs is a factor mainly during the early stages of treatment. Remember that the initial goal is to help patients stop using drugs completely and then help maintain that drug-free state. For that reason I encourage families of alcoholics to participate in Al-Anon, while I direct relatives of narcotic abusers to Nar-Anon. Al-Anon may also be of benefit to relatives of people who abuse tranquilizers. By taking part in a specialized program, families can learn the facts about the drug involved and its specific impact on the addict's mind, body, and behavior.

Another benefit is that families of a person who abuses one type of substance sometimes have difficulty relating to the problems faced by families of other types of addicts. For example, alcoholics abuse a legal substance, while cocaine users often run into trouble with the law. The impact of each of these drugs on a family's life can thus be quite different. A person's drug habit may have led to involvement with drug dealing. Many addicts rob or steal to pay for their drugs. Families in such circumstances need additional help; they may need to learn about legal services or other support services of which they can take advantage.

Several of my patients have also attended *Adult Children of Alcoholics* (ACOA) meetings. These ACOA have helped many adults to confront the difficult problems they encountered, and often tried to deny, when growing up in a family dominated by an alcoholic parent or parents. ACOA is one of the most astonishing movements of the last 10 years, with groups forming in virtually every section of the country.

In my part of the country, we are fortunate that programs such as Al-Anon and Nar-Anon are available. Although the situation is changing, such self-help groups may not exist where you live. If that is the case, check with your state or local Mental Health Association to find out if any other kinds of support groups are available. There may be a program aimed at spouses or significant others that focus on a particular substance of abuse or on issues related to social class or ethnicity. As a last resort you may want to work with local drug abuse specialists to organize a group of your own.

AGE

The patient's age has a direct impact on the type of family therapy offered. For younger drug abusers, therapy focuses on what is called the *family of origin*—parents, siblings, and so on. For older patients, the emphasis is on the *family of procreation*—the spouse or significant other and the children.

Most of my patients under 21 years of age are hooked on cocaine, followed by alcohol and then marijuana. In the 1970s, many of the young adults seeking treatment had a heroin problem; now the main drug of abuse in this age group is cocaine. For middle-age addicts, tranquilizers and alcohol are the most common problem. As the population ages, this picture will change; we'll begin to see more middle-aged and even elderly cocaine addicts in the coming years.

ETHNICITY

Ethnic background exerts a strong effect on the way a family functions. To a large extent, the way family members communicate among themselves and the roles they play are the product of tradition that may have been handed down over many generations. Among the factors we must explore as caregivers is how long the family has lived in America, the extent to which they have been assimilated in the mainstream of society, the ethnic composition of their neighborhood, and the extent to which members accept or reject their heritage. In considering ethnicity, though, we must keep in mind that regional differences also come into play. We can't, for example, lump all black patients into one group; it makes a difference whether a black patient comes from an urban community in the Northeast, a rural area of the South, or is a recent immigrant from Africa or the Caribbean. A good treatment program is sensitive to such issues and will resist stereotyping patients.

Generalizations are tricky, but we can see some relationship between ethnicity and the drug of choice involved. As a rule, white adolescents are more likely to abuse alcohol and marijuana, while nonwhite adolescents may be more involved in the use of heroin and barbiturates. (In the past five years or so, cocaine, especially in its crack form, seems to respect no boundaries of age or race.) Young people of Mexican-American heritage are more likely to abuse phencyclidine (PCP, or "angel dust"); Hispanic youths living on the East Coast tend to use inhalants.

As a drug treatment specialist, I try to be aware of some of the broader cultural issues that crop up. Again, stereotypes can be dangerous. But it is generally true that among certain people—for example, those of Italian-American descent—the family of origin is given top priority. Thus when an Italian woman marries into a family, she often finds herself competing with her husband's mother for his attention and affection. We may find that families have traditionally resisted coming into contact with the outside world—continuing to speak their native language, for example, or putting enormous pressure on offspring not to marry outside the culture or the religion. During therapy we look at the boundaries that exist between individuals and families and work on ways to change inappropriate or rigid boundaries and strengthen others.

Attitudes toward drugs, particularly alcohol, are often culturally generated and reinforced. The Italian community, for example, is generally intolerant of drunkenness, but it is not particularly concerned about drinking among young children. Partly as a result, the incidence of alcoholism among this group is lower than average.

Typically such families make it a "rule" not to discuss their dirty laundry in public. That may mean putting on masks in front of concerned others, including addiction therapists. Part of the job of treating such families involves building a sense of trust so that family members may discuss troublesome issues without feeling they are betraying one another or being disloyal.

Often, through therapy, the patient may discover that part of the problem stems from a family who prevents its children from breaking away and functioning confidently in the outside world. You may have heard some variation on this theme in your own family: "Why do you need to go to college in another state? There's a community college six blocks from here. You want to break your poor mother's heart, that's what you're trying to do." In group family sessions, such issues often crop up. Patients express their need to develop their own identities, while family members discover ways to let that happen without feeling that their internal bonds are threatened.

In contrast, the emphasis among Jewish-Americans tends to be placed more on the family of procreation. The boundaries in these families are often less rigid than those found in other cultures. This sometimes means that families are very democratic in their approach to solving problems. They may discuss problems quite openly, with every member, regardless of age, having some say in the matter. They often arrive at decisions by consensus rather than by decree. In treatment, once the therapist has earned their trust, Jewish families are usually willing to discuss problems openly and analyze them intellectually. The challenge is to move from talking about the need for change to bringing about change through action. If they are shown that change can happen without conflicting with their strong sense of values and tradition, the chances of success are greater.

When compared with other families, those who come from an Anglo-Saxon heritage tend to place a higher value on independence. Children are encouraged early on to strike out on their own and make their way in the world through hard work and initiative. The downside of this is that often such children lack a sense of belonging to an extended family. Once they leave their family of origin, they may lose contact with grandparents, cousins, even parents or siblings.

There is some truth to the stereotype of the WASP family members resisting the need to express their feelings, not just among themselves but within society as well. Another issue to contend with is the degree to which a person's sense of self-worth is tied into the work ethic. For some WASP substance abusers, their biggest problem may be their inability to hold a job or develop a meaningful career.

The cultural emphasis on individuality means that WASP families tend to perceive substance abuse as the patient's problem, not theirs, and thus find it difficult to ask for outside help. The challenge in therapy is to change that perception and encourage the family to take a more active role in supporting the patient. The addict in turn needs to learn to share feelings so that the family can understand what is happening, physically as well as emotionally. I've found that, as a rule, when these families are shown that treatment is a task that requires hard work but can produce clear and measurable results, they are often willing to commit themselves wholeheartedly to the process.

Another ethnic group with a distinct personality is the Irish-Americans. Because of their strong commitment to their religious heritage, such families tend to see drug therapy as a form of confession, in which sins are admitted and forgiveness is sought. The problem is that religious confession is a private matter, while therapy that calls for working through problems in the presence of other families, which can provoke feelings of embarrassment. In contrast to the Italian heritage, among the Irish drunkenness is more likely to be tolerated whereas drinking by children is not, a trait that may contribute to the fact that alcoholism is more prevalent among this group than other ethnic types.

On the whole, Irish families tend to be dominated by the mother. The challenge is thus to get the father involved in therapy as much as possible. In my experience, these families tend to feel somewhat uncomfortable in therapy. Nonetheless they feel a deep sense of personal responsibility toward each other. I find that these families will continue to work on their problems on their own, long after the formal treatment program has ended.

For African-American families, the problems of racism and discrimination have a pronounced impact on the course and effectiveness of therapy. Some urban blacks have come to perceive that drug dealing is their ticket out of the ghetto. Often, few role models exist to counteract this impression. In a number of black families, the mother is the only parent available. Because the mother is forced to work, she may be absent from the home for long periods, which often means a grandmother or other relative is called on to help raise the children. It can be very hard for a mother struggling to put food on the table to tell her son to stop giving her grocery money that she knows came from the sale of drugs. Thus, lacking strong social and family support, many black addicts are unable to take advantage of family therapy. But as I've said often throughout this book, a treatment program that doesn't address family concerns has a far lower chance of working. When the family of a black patient does agree to take part, it seems that they generally respond better to an approach that concentrates on strengthening the family structure than on talk therapy or other strategies.

OTHER ISSUES

Aside from ethnicity, each family develops its own personality and style of interacting. These traits become most apparent when the family is forced to deal with a crisis, such as a substance-abusing member. There are basically four types of families—which of these best describes your family?

Functional families present an image of order and stability to the outside world while working furiously behind the scenes to maintain that image. These families seem to have no conflicts and appear to be successful and stable. Because they are organized to defend the status quo, such families tend to resist the insights that family therapy can provide: "There's nothing wrong with us. Why should we talk about non-existent problems in a roomful of strangers?" When I deal with such families, I find that they respond best when we emphasize factual information about drug abuse and the medical problems it can cause. Handled properly, such a strategy helps them realize the consequences of addiction and the need to support the person with the drug problem. In the process the family learns about the rules by which they have been operating, and can begin to change those rules that may have contributed to the current difficulty. Such families tend to resist exploring their emotions and discovering how their feelings affect their interactions with each other. Instead, they usually do better when treatment is aimed at changing their faulty patterns of thinking.

Enmeshed families are those where the members are tightly bound up with one another, emotionally as well as physically. As a rule, we often find a high degree of codependency and enabling among members of an enmeshed family. That means therapy may be more difficult and prolonged. Remember that codependents may resist helping the patient end the addiction, since the entire family has become organized around that problem. Patients from enmeshed families are at highest risk of relapse. During therapy we concentrate on the need to reinforce family boundaries, define each individual's role within the family, and reduce their overly sensitive reactivity to one another. Since therapy with such families tends to be long-term, we take particular care to steer them into Twelve-Step or other support groups.

Disintegrated families, as the name suggests, have fallen apart through separation, divorce, or death—often as a direct result of substance abuse and not its cause. Thus treatment in such cases, especially early in the process, may involve only the patient and no one else. Our primary goal in such cases is to help the patient become drug-free and stay that way for a period of time. Once we can show the other family members that we've made some progress, they may be more willing to assume a role in therapy. If we somehow manage to bring together members of a disintegrated family, much of our time will be devoted to dealing with the intense feelings of anger and hostility—or, worse, apathy—that the patient and the addiction evoke. On rare occasions families are able patch up their differences and get back together. Although that's a desirable outcome, it isn't really the goal.

Absent families are ones where patients have no contact with their families and lack other permanent relationships as well. In such cases—challenging ones, I admit—we try to contact friends and members of the extended family to strength the patient's sense of social support. Particularly if such patients are young, we will try to connect them to a peer-group network, such as a long-term therapeutic community, a Twelve-Step program, a church outreach program, or some other organization. The hope is that the patient can develop social skills and build a new life, even in the absence of strong family ties.

SPECIAL NEEDS OF WOMEN

For too long now, treatment for substance abuse has generally been oriented to meet the needs of men. I've found this troublesome, since as a rule chemically dependent women and their families are much worse off. Such families tend to have more than one substance-abusing member; there is a higher incidence of mental illness, suicide, violence, physical abuse, and sexual abuse. Unfortunately, many treatment programs refuse to deal with women, especially if she is pregnant, and pathetically few programs make any kind of provision for child care. Thus a woman who recognizes that she needs help may not be able to find it; even if she does, the courts may take her children away from her and place them in foster care.

The arrival of crack cocaine has made matters worse. For some hideous reason, crack is far more appealing to women than other drugs. We thus have many crack-addicted women, many of whom continue to smoke the drug even after they become pregnant. I know of more than one case where the woman smoked on her way to the delivery room! The tragic result is that many babies—in some areas, estimates range to as high as one in five or even one in three—are born already addicted to cocaine. The sad thought often crosses my mind that some of these will become my patients in just a few years.

Statistics show that when a marriage splits up due to substance abuse, nine out of ten times it is because the man leaves an addicted woman. In only one out of ten cases does the woman abandon the addicted man. Thus far more women addicts suffer the loss of a mate than their male counterparts. If the woman is unable to support herself and her family financially, she then risks losing custody of her children. Surveys show that a significant percentage of female substance abusers are victims of incest, battering, or rape.

For these and other reasons, family therapy is especially vital when the identified patient is a woman. If you are looking for a treatment program for a female relative, be especially sure that therapists are sensitive to women's problems and are willing to confront these issues head-on in therapy. If you sense that the caregivers have a stereotyped view of women and their roles in today's society, *run, don't walk,* to another program.

Also, make sure the program offers therapy sessions open to women only. Such sessions make it possible for patients to express their feelings more openly than if men were present, increasing the likelihood that the woman will experience the emotional catharsis that serves as a prelude to beginning life anew.

SPECIAL NEEDS OF OLDER INDIVIDUALS

All too often our society tends to consider addiction as a problem among the young, and thus will overlook the problem of substance abuse among the middle-aged and elderly. In some cases, the use of chemicals may have gone on for so long that no one remembers what the person was like before the addiction, and thus will fail to recognize the problem. In other cases, the symptoms of drug or alcohol abuse may be masked by some other psychiatric or medical problem, such as depression, a chronic infection, or Alzheimer's. Members of older generations, who grew up in an era when addiction or alcoholism were viewed as moral failings, are more likely to deny that they have a substance abuse problem for fear of social ostracism. In many cases, older people are given prescription after prescription—diuretics, antidepressants, sleeping pills. They continue using their medications for years, even after the condition has cleared up. Yet doctors frequently fail to update their medical records, although in doing so they would spot out-of-date or unnecessary prescriptions.

Another factor is that, for older generations, the drug of choice is usually alcohol. There are statistically very few cocaine abusers over the age of, say, 45. Because alcohol is legal, and because drinking habits may have been ingrained for decades, it may be very hard to get the person to admit a problem and then intervene effectively to steer the person into treatment.

Family treatment of elderly patients is, ironically, in its infancy. Sometimes an older patient's access to therapy is limited by the constraints of the Medicare system. Many facilities, including my own hospital, can only afford to accept elderly patients who have private insurance, since reimbursement under Medicare wouldn't even begin to cover the costs of treatment.

Family therapy for the elderly must, almost by definition, include the children. Not long ago, for instance, my hospital treated a 96-year-old alcoholic (yes, he had private medical coverage) who was brought into treatment by his 72-year-old daughter who was concerned that he would fall and injure himself. Sometimes it is equally important, if not more so, to involve the grandchildren as well. In many cases elderly patients who may have cut themselves off from their own children will respond to a show of concern from their grandchildren.

Ideally therapy will offer group discussions among people of similar age. The elderly may be wrestling with feelings of despair, futility, hopelessness, or failure that a 20-year-old, for example, may not relate to on any level whatsoever. The goal is to show older patients that no matter how troubled their family relationships may have been till now, there is always a chance for change, and that their remaining years, whatever their number, may still be filled with happiness.

As I hope I've shown in this book, addiction is a complex problem that requires complex solutions. Drugs are dangerous, not just because they affect the person who abuses them but because they destroy whole families as well. In their effort to get better, chemically dependent people need the most powerful medicine of all: the love of their family. Often, in the midst of suffering, a family forgets how to communicate.

When the family shares the addict's burden, the road to recovery—often long and seldom smooth—becomes much easier to travel.

SOURCES

Ciraulo, Domenic A.; Barnhill, Jamie G.; Ciraulo, Ann Marie, et al: "Parental Alcoholism as a Risk Factor in Benzodiazepine Abuse: A Pilot Study," *American Journal of Psychiatry* 146:1333–35, October 10, 1989.

Cloninger, C. Robert; Dinwiddie, Stephen H., and Reich, Theodore: Tasman, A.; Hales, R., and Fraces, A. eds.: "Epidemiology and Genetics of Alcoholism." *In: Review of Psychiatry,* Volume 8. Washington, D.C.: American Psychiatric Press, 1989, pp. 293–308.

Cloninger, C. Robert; Sigvardsson, Soren; Gilligan, Shelia B., et al: "Genetic Heterogeneity and the Classification of Alcoholism," *Advances in Alcohol and Substance Abuse* 7(3/4):3–16, 1988.

Dackis, Charles A.; Gold, Mark S., and Estroff, Todd W.: "Inpatient Treatment of Addiction." *In: Treatments of Psychiatric Disorders: A Task Force Report of the American Psychiatric Association.* Karasu, T. B., ed. Washington, D.C.: American Psychiatric Association, 1989: pp 1359–79.

Dackis, Charles A., and Gold, Mark S.: "Alcoholism." *In:* Gold, Mark S.; Lydiard, R. Bruce, and Carman, John S., eds.: *Advances in Psychopharmacology: Predicting and Improving Treatment Response.* Boca Raton, Fla.: CRC Press, 1986, pp. 277–88.

DeMilio, Lawrence; Gold, Mark S., and Martin, David: "Evaluation of the Substance Abuser." *In:* Gold, Mark S., and Pottash, A.L.C., eds.: *Diagnostic and Laboratory Testing in Psychiatry.* New York: Plenum Medical Book Company, 1986, pp. 235–47.

Diagram Group: *The Brain: A User's Manual.* New York: Berkley Books, 1983.

Extein, Irl; Dackis, Charles A.; Gold, Mark S., and Pottash, A.L.C.: "Depression in Drug Addicts and Alcoholics." *In:* Extein, Irl, and Gold, Mark S., eds.: *Medical Mimics of Psychiatric Disorders.* Washington, D.C.: American Psychiatric Press, 1986, pp. 131–62.

Extein, Irl L.: "An Update on Cocaine," *Currents* 7(2):5–13, February 1988.

Friel, John, and Friel, Linda: *Adult Children: The Secrets of Dysfunctional Families.* Deerfield Beach, Fla.: Health Communications, Inc., 1988.

Gold, Mark S.: *The Facts About Drugs and Alcohol, Third Revised Edition.* New York: Bantam Books, 1988.

Goodwin, Donald W.; Schulsinger, Fini; Knop, Joachim, et al.: "Alcoholism and Depression in Adopted-Out Daughters of Alcoholics," *Archives of General Psychiatry* 34:751–55, July 1977.

Henricks, Lorraine: *Kids Who Do/Kids Who Don't: A Parent's Guide to Teens and Drugs.* Summit, N.J.: PIA Press, 1989.

Kaufman, Edward F.: "Family Therapy in Substance Abuse Treatment." *In: Treatments of Psychiatric Disorders: A Task Force Report of the American Psychiatric Association.* Washington, D.C.: American Psychiatric Association, 1989, pp. 1397–1417.

Kline, David: "The Anatomy of Addiction," *Equinox* 4(23):77–86, September/October 1985.

Linnoila, Markku: "Neurotransmitters and Alcoholism: Methodological Issues," *Advances in Alcohol and Substance Abuse* 7(3/4):17–24, 1988.

Milam, James R., and Ketcham, Katherine: *Under the Influence.* New York: Bantam Books, 1983.

Miller, Norman S., and Gold, Mark S.: "Research Approaches to Inheritance to Alcoholism, *Substance Abuse.* [in press] 1990.

Mirin, Steven M., and Weiss, Roger D.: "Genetic Factors in the Development of Alcoholism," *Psychiatric Annals* 19(5):239–42, May 1989.

Mumey, Jack: *Loving an Alcoholic.* New York: Bantam Books, 1988.

Munjack, Dennis J., and Moss, Howard B.: "Affective Disorder and Alcoholism in Families of Agoraphobics," *Archives of General Psychiatry;* 38:869–71, August 1981.

Nace, Edgar P.: "Personality Disorder in the Alcoholic Patient," *Psychiatric Annals* 19(5):256–60, May 1989.

Robertson, Nan: *Getting Better: Inside Alcoholics Anonymous.* New York: Fawcett Crest, 1988.

Schuckit, Marc A.: "Familial Alçoholism," *Vista Hill Foundation Drug Abuse & Alcoholism Newsletter* 18(9):1–4, November 1989.

Weiss, Roger D., and Mirin, Steven M.: "The Dual Diagnosis Alcoholic: Evaluation and Treatment," *Psychiatric Annals* 19(5):261–65, May 1989.

Yandow, Valery: "Alcoholism in Women," *Psychiatric Annals* 19(5):243–47, May 1989.

INDEX

AA (Alcoholics Anonymous)
  biology of addiction and, 47-49
  defense mechanisms and, 43-44
  founders of, 47
  membership of, 47
  philosophy of, 47
  strategies of, 47-49
  Twelve-Step programs of, 14, 18, 48, 87, 91-94
Absent families, 125
Abstinence, 89
ACOA (Adult Children of Alcoholics), 117
Acquaintances, 65
Addiction
  biology of
    AA and, 47-49
    destiny and, 55-56
    disease model, 45-47
    genetics and, 49-51, 52
    physical process of, 51-53
    stages of, 53-55
  cases of, 1-4, 8

cold medications and, 97
community leaders and, 27-28
complexity of, 128-129
cycle of, 1-3
defense mechanisms in
  behavioral, 31
  cognitive, 31-32
  compensation, 38-39
  denial, 32-36
  dual diagnosis and, 39-43
  emotional, 32
  family therapy and, 43-44
  intellectualization, 37-38
  projection, 38-39
  rationalization, 36-37
  splitting, 39
  types of, 30-32
denial of, 28, 30-31
as disease, 13, 47
doctors and, 27-28
education about, 63
employers and, 26-27
factors of, 72

134

family and, 6-9
friends and, 26
hospitalization for, 75-76
intervention in
  case of, 57-58
  process of, 61-69
  resistance to, 59-61
love triangle and, 14
parents and, 24-25
people affected by, 5
pressure and, 5-6
recovery from, 13-14
relapse and, 101-103
stages of, 53-55
substance of abuse and, 13
as symptom of psychiatric disorder, 13
systems approach to, 9-11
therapy and, 11-14
victims of, 7
Adult Children of Alcoholics
  (ACOA), 117
African-Americans, 122-123
Age, 117-118
Alanon, 43-44, 92, 117
Alateen, 92
Alcohol abuse, 22-23, 40-42, 49-50.
  See also Substance abuse
Alcohol addiction, 17-18, 49,
  51. See also Addiction
Alcoholics Anonymous. See AA
Alcoholism. See Alcohol addic-
  tion
Alprazolam, 42
Anger, 104
Anglo-Saxons, 121-122
Antidepressants, 42
Anxiety, 11, 41

Behavioral strategies, 31
Benzodiazepines, 42
Biopsychosocial model, 9-11, 19
Bipolar I, 41
Bipolar II, 41
Bipolar mood disorder, 41
Brain, 52-53

Castles in the clouds, 105-106
Chemical dependency. See Addiction; Substance abuse
Cocaine abuse, 36-37, 55, 109,
  126-127. See also Substance
  abuse
Coc-Anon, 92
Codependency
  awareness of, 17-18
  cases of, 15-16, 22-24
  confusion about, 17-18
  definition of, 6, 20
  enabling and, 20-22
  evolution of, 18-20
  family and, 18
  parents and, 24-25
  publicity of, 28-29
  sides to, 20-21
  social factors in, 26-29
Codependents, 19, 20
Cognitive strategies,
  31-32
Coke dreams, 109
Cold medications, 97
Communication, 77, 79, 110
Community leaders, 27-28
Compensation, 38-39
Consolidation, 90-91
Crack, 36-37, 126. See also Cocaine abuse
Crusading, 106-107

Defense mechanisms
  AA and, 43-44
  behavioral, 31
  cognitive, 31-32
  definition of, 31
  denial, 32-36
  dual diagnosis and, 39-43
  emotional, 32
  family therapy and, 43-44
  intellectualization, 37-38
  projection, 38-39
  rationalization, 36-37
  splitting, 39
  types of, 31-32

Denial
  of addiction, 28, 30-31
  as defense mechanism, 32-36
  differences in types of, 33
  by doctors, 34-35
  by employers, 34
  by parents of addicts, 33-34
  problem of, 28
  of relapse, 90
  by spouses, 34
  statements of, 33
  of substance abuse, 22, 35-36
Dependency, 13, 54. *See also* Addiction
Depression, 11, 41-42
Discipline, lack of, 107-108
Disease model, 45-47, 53
Disintegrated families, 124-125
Divorce, 7, 127
Doctors, 27-28, 34-35, 64-65
Dopamine, 36-37
Drug abuse. *See also* Cocaine abuse; Substance abuse
  abstinence and, 89
  case of, 1-4, 23-24
  conditioned response and, 89-90
  in families, 12
  mood swings in, 41
  therapy for, 5
"Drug pushing", 107
"Dry home", 95-100
Dual diagnosis, 39-43
Dysfunctional families, 13

Elderly, 127-128
Emotional strategies, 32
Emotions, 12
Employers, 26-27, 34, 64
Enabling
  behaviors, 21
  case of, 16
  codependency and, 20-22
  definition of, 21
  family and, 24-25
  parents and, 24-25
Enmeshed families, 124

Entrained behavior, 53
Ethnicity, 118-123
Experimental stage, 53-54

Familial alcoholism, 49-50
Family
  absent, 125
  addiction and, 6-9
  alcoholism in, 49-50
  changes in, 12-13
  codependency and, 18
  concept of, 6-9
  definition of, 7
  disintegrated, 124-125
  divorce and, 7
  drug abuse in, 12
  dysfunctional, 13
  enabling and, 24-25
  enmeshed, 124
  functional, 123-124
  in inpatient setting, 6, 70-72
  intervention and, 64
  love given by, 14
  in outpatient setting, 6, 84-85, 95-100
  recovery and, 85, 95-100
  substance abuse and, 6-9, 123-125
  substance abuse in, 12
  therapy and, 8
  types of, and family therapy, 123-125
Family of origin, 117-118
Family of procreation, 118, 120
Family therapy. *See also* Inpatient setting; Outpatient setting; Therapy
  age and, 117-118
  cases of, 113-115
  defense mechanisms and, 43-44
  drug treatment and, 25
  effective, 74-77
  elderly and, 127-128
  ethnicity and, 118-123
  factors affecting, 115-116
  family type and, 123-125

goal of, 43
levels of work of, 71
multifamily therapy and, 80-81
process of, 71-72, 77-81
shopping for, 72-74
strategy for, 76-77
substance of abuse and, 116-117
women and, 125-127
Feelings, 12
Friends, 26, 65
Functional families, 123-124

Genetics, 49-51, 52

Halfway houses, 86
Hospitalization, 75-76. *See also*
Inpatient setting
Hospitals. *See* Inpatient setting
Hunger, 103

ID (identified patient), 71-72, 74,
78
Identified patient, *See* ID
Imipramine, 40-41
Inpatient setting
effective, 74-77
family in, 6, 70-72
final phase of, 81-83
process of, 77-81
shopping for, 72-74
Intellectualization, 37-38
Intervention
case of, 57-58
definition of, 6
goal of, 62
process of
follow-up support in, 68-69
participants in, 64-65
preparation for, 62-63
professional help in, 61-62
script for, 66-68
setting of, 65-66
resistance to, 59-61
Irish-Americans, 122

Jewish-Americans, 120-121

Librium, 42
Limbic system, 52-53
Lithium, 41
Loneliness, 104
Love triangle, 14

Magical thinking, 105
Medical professionals, 27-28. *See
also* Doctors
Mental disorder, 40-42
Methadone maintenance pro-
grams, 86
Mood swings, 41
Multifamily therapy, 80-81

Nar-Anon, 92, 117
Nonverbal communication, 79
Nutrition, 54

Outpatient clinic, 86
Outpatient setting
effective, 87-89
family in, 6, 84-85, 95-100
phases of treatment in, 89-91
twelve-step approach to, 91-94
types of, 85-87
Overconfidence, 104-105

Parents, 24-25, 33-34
Physicians. *See* Doctors
Pressure, 5-6
Projection, 38

Quality time, 12-13

Rationalization, 36-37
Recovery
from addiction, 13-14
definition of, 6
family and, 85, 95-100
Relapse
addiction and, 101-103
definition of, 6
denial of, 90
therapy and, 108-112
warning signs of, 103-108

Residential therapeutic communities, 86
Resistance, to intervention, 59-61

Self-help groups, 43-44, 111. *See also* specific names of
Self-pity, 106
Splitting, 39
Sponsors, 111
Spouses, 34
Substance abuse. *See also* Addiction
  addiction and, 13
  age and, 118
  attitudes about, 35-36, 119-120
  cases of, 1-4, 8
  choice of, 35-36, 116-117
  denial of, 22, 35-36
  dual diagnosis and, 42
  elderly and, 127-128
  ethnicity and, 118-123
  in families, 12
  family and, 6-9, 123-125
  genetics and, 49-51, 52
  mental disorder and, 40-42
  nutrition and, 54
  people affected by, 5
  physical process and, 51-53
  secrecy in, 22

severity of, 115-116
stages of, 53-55
systems approach to, 9-11
tolerance in, 54
toleration of, 28
women and, 125-127
Systems approach, 9-11

Therapy. *See also* Family therapy
  addiction and, 11-14
  benefits of, 9
  for drug abuse, 5
  as education, 11-14
  family and, 8
  relapse and, 108-112
  systems approach to, 9-11
Tiredness, 104
Tolerance, 54
Toleration, 28
Tranquilizers, 42
Twelve-Step programs. *See* AA

Valium, 42

WASPs, 121-122
Women, 125-127

Xanax, 42